William Spon Baker

The Engraved Portraits of Washington

William Spon Baker

The Engraved Portraits of Washington

ISBN/EAN: 9783744677530

Printed in Europe, USA, Canada, Australia, Japan

Cover: Foto ©Thomas Meinert / pixelio.de

More available books at **www.hansebooks.com**

THE ENGRAVED

PORTRAITS OF WASHINGTON,

WITH

NOTICES OF THE ORIGINALS AND BRIEF BIOGRAPHICAL
SKETCHES OF THE PAINTERS.

BY

W. S. BAKER,

Author of "The Antiquity of Engraving and The Utility and Pleasures of Prints;"
"William Sharp, Engraver, and his Works;" and "American
Engravers and their Works."

PHILADELPHIA:
LINDSAY & BAKER.
1880.

PREFACE.

THE present work, although somewhat broader in its scope than others of a similar character, was compiled simply as a Text-book for the Washington collector.

To an American no other portrait can possess the interest and significance which will be always attached to that of Washington; and if in contemplating it, we feel impressed with the nobility of his character, the dignity of his manhood, his truth and patriotism, what better page can we study and what better life can we imitate ?

The portraits of Washington are fortunately not restricted to a single example nor limited to the individual painter, and while extending over the greater portion of his life, cover more particularly the years devoted to his country. If it is true that "a portrait is a sort of general history of the person it represents," how complete must be that history when fully presented in a regular series, and brought through the medium of the graver to our quiet and careful consideration.

Quite a number of collections of the engraved portraits of Washington have been gathered and some of considerable importance, but as yet no system of arrangement has been attempted by which the prints, although always interesting in themselves, could be intelligently studied either historically or artistically.

With the view, therefore, of making such collections instructive,

something more than merely interesting, the system has been adopted
of classifying the prints according to the painters, and by furnishing a
chronological series of, with but one or two exceptions, all the known
originals, give at a glance a concise history of the subject.   No other
form can so thoroughly enable the student to comprehend the different
types of portraits with the period of production, and allow him through
his prints to follow the career of " our Washington," and while considering the acts and results of his life, be, at the same time, forcibly
reminded of the prominent events of the early history of the Republic,
which although comparatively recent in date, we, in the rapid changes
of the present, already look back upon with a feeling of antiquity, but
not, we hope, in a spirit of forgetfulness.

As indispensable to the proper understanding of the engraved portraits, brief biographical sketches of the painters have been given,
restricted as much as possible to the special subject under consideration, which will serve to draw attention to a few originals, not as yet
reproduced by the burin, but completing the historical series.

With the exception of the lithographic drawings by Rembrandt
Peale, and the one copied from the original etching by Joseph Wright,
noticed in consequence of the endorsement certifying to its correctness
as a likeness, the catalogue is restricted to the record of the productions of *plate* engravers only, the large number of wood-cuts and litho-
graphs precluding their admission even if desirable or customary,
although many are close renderings of originals and moreover possess
considerable artistic merit.

In arranging the prints according to painters more or less difficulty
was encountered, it being apparent in some cases that the engraver

had worked from no authentic original, the plate being produced either from irresponsible pictures and drawings or other engravings no better entitled to consideration. This necessarily required careful comparison and examination, and from the fact that a number of prints were not available for that purpose, some assignments may be open to objection; it is hoped, however, that in this respect but few errors will be discovered.

A chronological arrangement of the prints in each list would have been the most natural and satisfactory, but the impossibility of obtaining dates of publication of many, rendered this impracticable, and the alphabetical plan was adopted, which in the end renders the catalogue more convenient for reference and enables each engraver's productions, when after the same original, to follow in consecutive order. This has, however, been departed from whenever there existed original prints by any of the painters, as in the case of the plates by Charles Wilson Peale, Joseph Wright, Edward Savage, and Saint Memin, and the drawings on stone by Rembrandt Peale above referred to, these forming for such lists the appropriate headings.

All the prints enumerated in the catalogue have come under the immediate notice of the writer, with but two exceptions, one engraved by Norman after Charles Willson Peale, and the other by Hamlin, No. 125, a copy of the mezzotinto by Savage, the first named being in the possession of C. W. Folsom, of Cambridge, Mass., and the latter in the collection of James E. Mauran, of Newport, R. I., to which gentlemen we are indebted for the respective descriptions.

The book-plates have been ascribed to the work in which they were originally published, whenever such information was obtainable, and any omission in this respect it is hoped will be supplied by the interested collector.

The designations *rare, very rare,* and *extremely rare,* have been used with much caution, and the term *unique* entirely discarded. The rarity of a print is a matter somewhat difficult to determine, and at best the use of the terms above mentioned becomes to a greater or lesser extent arbitrary in character. In establishing a rule for their application we have been entirely governed by actual observation and the experience derived from the knowledge of impressions which occur in important collections, and not from the difficulty experienced in obtaining them at present from the folio of the dealer.

The word *unique,* which may in some instances be properly applied to an impression from a particular state of the plate not intended to be published, cannot with close adherence to truth be used in referring to those taken for the regular edition, no matter how few in number, as it is scarcely probable, especially as to any Washington print, that all have disappeared save one only, and though the possessor is likely in his enthusiasm to declare to the contrary, others sooner or later will come to the surface. Those prints of which only one impression has as yet come under the notice of the writer have been marked accordingly, but the designation *unique* has been studiously avoided.

A number of prints, from having no means of identification either by title, inscription, or names of engraver or publisher, were omitted, it seeming to be useless to record what could not be discovered either by index or otherwise, the list of anonymous being already much larger than was desirable.

In all the descriptions, *the right* and *the left*, it will be understood refer to the right and the left of the observer, as the print is held directly before him.

Apart from the compiler's own collection, the material for the cata-
logue was obtained from those, formed by the following gentlemen:
Thomas A. Emmet, M.D., Edward Dexter, Joseph A. Drexel, John B.
Moreau, Charles C. Moreau, William A. Fraser, Henry T. Drowne, and
William L. Andrews, of New York; and R. Coulton Davis, Simon
Gratz, Ferdinand J. Dreer, Frederick D. Stone, Henry Whelen, Jr.,
Howard Edwards, and Charles Henry Hart, of Philadelphia; to all of
whom he is extremely indebted, for opportunities offered, courteous
attention, and aid in examination. To the latter named gentleman,
however, something more than mere thanks is due, and we take this
opportunity of publicly recognizing our estimation, of his valuable
assistance, and practical counsel, constantly given through the progress of the work, the value of which only those familiar with the
difficulties of such an undertaking can fully appreciate.

Each one of the collections above mentioned, contains more or less
matter which does not exist in the others, the most complete in a
general way being that of Mr. Dexter, and the greatest rarities being
comprised in Dr. Emmet's.

W. S. BAKER.

PHILADELPHIA, Nov. 1, 1879.

2

CHARLES WILLSON PEALE.

1772–95.

The painter of the first authentic portrait of Washington, was born of English parents at Chestertown, on the Eastern Shore of Maryland, April 15, 1741. At the age of twenty-one, having served his time with a saddler of Annapolis, he commenced for himself, combining with his trade several others, such as coach-making, and clock and watch-making, besides working as a silversmith, and finally trying his hand at portrait painting. In the latter pursuit he had some little advice, a handsome saddle being the consideration, from a Mr. Hesselius, an Englishman, who married and settled in Annapolis in the year 1763.

After a brief visit to Boston, where he was kindly received by J. Singleton Copley, then established as a portrait painter, and who gave him some instruction, Peale determined upon a voyage to London, and being assisted by several gentlemen of Annapolis, the loan to be repaid by pictures, sailed for England, arriving in London in the summer of 1768. Benjamin West received him into his house, and he studied during 1768–69 in the Royal Academy under that painter's direction, at the same time turning his attention to painting in miniature, and engraving in mezzotinto.

On his return in June, 1770, he set up his easel as a portrait painter at Annapolis and Baltimore, finding constant employment and gaining considerable reputation. The fame of the young painter reached Mount

Vernon, and he was invited there to delineate for the first time, the form and features of the proprietor.

This picture, painted in May, 1772, a three-quarter length, represents Washington in the costume of a Colonel of the 22d Regiment of Virginia Militia; a blue coat faced with red, bright metal buttons having the number of the regiment cast upon them, and dark red waistcoat and breeches. He wears the hat usually called the Wolfe hat, with sash and gorget. This has been engraved by Steel, Paradise, Parker, Forrest, Rogers, and Buttre.

Peale remained at Mount Vernon several weeks, and painted portraits in miniature of the different members of the family. He finally settled at Philadelphia.

In the summer of 1776, having joined the army as a Captain of Volunteers, Peale painted a half-length portrait of the Commander-in-chief for John Hancock (engraved by Norman), and in December, 1777, completed a miniature for Mrs. Washington. It was begun at the close of October. While sitting for it at a farm house near Skippack Creek, Pennsylvania, the General (who occupied the side of a bed and the artist the only chair in the small room) received dispatches advising him of the capture of Burgoyne, which he merely glanced at, and then remained apparently unconcerned until the sitting was finished. An engraving by De Mare from this miniature, or from a copy made by Peale himself, is published in Irving's Life of Washington, without being ascribed to the painter, and with the erroneous title, "Washington at the age of twenty-five."

A sketch, inscribed "Pencel (*sic*) sketch of General Washington from life taken by Chas. Willson Peale 1777," in possession of the "Historical Society of Pennsylvania," resembles somewhat this engraving. It is a bust in uniform, slightly executed, inclosed in a border resting upon a base, and seems to have been drawn for the purpose of being engraved. Including the border it is 5 4-16 inches in height by 4 12-16 inches in width.

Congress having passed a resolution previous to the occupation of Philadelphia by the British army, ordering a portrait of the Commander-in-chief, Peale commenced it at Valley Forge in the spring of 1778. Soon after the first sitting, the troops left Valley Forge, and pursued the British in their flight from Philadelphia toward New York. The painter took his materials with him, participated in the battle of Monmouth at the close of June, and a day or two afterward, procured another sitting at New Brunswick. The picture was finally completed at Philadelphia; Nassau Hall, Princeton, is a prominent object in the background.

Congress adjourned without making an appropriation, and the picture remained with the artist until his decease, when it passed into private hands. A copy of it, signed and dated Philadelphia, 1779, was afterwards sent to Europe for sale; it became the property of the Count de Menou, who brought it to the United States and presented it to the National Institute. It is now in possession of the Smithsonian Institution. The engraving by Wolff, a good rendering of the picture and accurate in detail, was most probably executed from this copy. Another copy, painted about the same time, intended as a present to the Stadtholder, was captured in 1780 with Henry Laurens on his passage to Holland, by Captain Keppel of the British Navy, who gave it to his uncle, Admiral Lord Keppel. It is now at Quidenham Park, Norfolk,

England, the seat of the Earl of Albemarle, the present head of the Keppel family.

Peale also painted in 1778 a miniature of Washington, for Lafayette; of this he made several copies.

In the winter of 1778–79, Washington being in Philadelphia for a short time, sat at the request of the Council of State (Pa.) to Peale, for a whole length, to be placed in the Council Chamber. From this he seems to have executed a plate in mezzotinto, as appears by the following advertisement in "The Pennsylvania Packet, or the General Advertiser," published at Philadelphia Saturday, August 26, 1780. "The subscriber takes this method of informing the public that he has just finished a metzotinto print in poster size (14 inches by 10 inches besides the margin) of His Excellency General Washington, from the original picture belonging to the State of Pennsylvania. Shopkeepers, and persons going to the West Indies, may be supplied at such a price as will afford a considerable profit to them, by applying at the Southwest corner of Lombard and Third Streets, Philadelphia. Charles Willson Peale."

This was repeated on September 9th, and with a slight variation on December 6th and 26th of the same year; in these the price, two dollars, being given. No impression of this print, notwithstanding the most diligent inquiry, has come under the notice of the writer. This picture was afterwards (1781), defaced and totally destroyed, by some persons who broke into the Council Chamber, whether from malice or in a wanton spirit of destruction does not appear.

In 1780 Peale painted another whole length, under the following circumstances: At the battle of Princeton, January 3, 1777, when Washington opened fire upon Nassau Hall (occupied by the enemy), the first cannon ball which entered the building passed through the head of a portrait of George II. suspended in a large frame upon the wall. It is alleged that Washington in order to make good to the College the damage sustained by the cannonade, made the Trustees a present from his private purse of two hundred and fifty dollars, which sum they expended in procuring a whole length portrait of the Commander-in-chief, placing it in the identical frame in which hung the king's portrait. In the background is seen Nassau Hall and a sketch of the battle of Princeton, and to the right the figure of General Mercer mortally wounded. There is no engraving of this picture, but it has been reproduced on wood, for illustration. (Lossing's Pictorial Field-book of the Revolution, vol. ii. p. 37.)

In the year 1783 he painted a whole length for the State of Maryland; in this he introduced portraits of Lafayette and Colonel Tilghman. The picture was in commemoration of the surrender at Yorktown, and represents the continental army passing in review. This has not been engraved.

In the following year (1784), Peale painted to the order of the Governor of Virginia another whole length. This was intended to be used by the sculptor Houdon, in preparing his model for the statue ordered by the State; but arrangements were subsequently made, which enabled him to visit the country, and make an actual cast from the head, and measurements of the person of Washington himself. Peale in his letter dated Philadelphia, October 30, 1784, advising the Governor of its completion, and his purpose of sending it by the first vessel going to France, says: " Besides the view of York and Gloster as mentioned in a former letter, I have introduced on a near ground French and American officers with their colors *displayed*, and between them the British with their colors *cased;* these figures seem to tell the story at first sight, which the more distant could not. P. S. The price of a coppy *(sic)* of Genl. Washington in large whole length is thirty guineas, and the packing case three dollars." It is not known what became of this picture.

In 1786 Peale painted a portrait of Washington, head-size, for his Gallery. This is the portrait referred to by his son Rembrandt in his lecture on " Washington and his Portraits," during the sittings for which he stood behind his father's chair.

The mezzotinto plate first described in the appended list, was executed in 1787. It has no particular artistic merit, but possesses considerable interest as an original work, although, in character and drawing, different from other originals familiar to us.

Peale painted fourteen portraits of Washington from life, the last in the autumn of 1795. This is now in the Gallery of the " New York Historical Society."

Charles Willson Peale died at Philadelphia February 22, 1827.

Quite a number of the prints in the following list executed by foreign engravers, are extremely unsatisfactory, as renderings of any of the Washington portraits painted by Peale. The miniature executed for Lafayette in 1778, was possibly the first portrait known abroad, and seems to have been at once taken hold of and either copied or used as a groundwork, for the production of pictures calculated to please the popular taste. From these copies and pictures, engravings were made and repeated again and again, losing naturally in every step, the force and character of the original. This is proved by Lavater, who in his remarks upon the one published in the French edition of his Essay on Physiognomy, (afterwards copied by Holloway for the English edition and also by Zerlamsler,) says, "If Washington is the author of the revolution, we have seen him undertake and accomplish with so much success, it is positive that the designer must have lost some of the most striking features of the original." The outline by Halder in the same work, which resembles very closely the head in the print by Norman, seems to have, however, thoroughly satisfied the physiognomist, as he found in it all the characteristics which were wanting in the other.

The engraving by Le Mire, full length, is from a made-up picture; this is copied with slight variations in those published in England by Carington Bowles, and Laurie & Whittle, while the head appears in those executed by Angus, Cook, and J. L., and the one published by Thom. Hart. The engraving by Sharp, copied by Pruneau, and repeated as to the head, by Carey and Newton, and in the one published by Whitworth & Yates, was made from a print obtained in Paris, and altered to suit the fancy of the author of the work in which it appeared, each reproduction removing it further from the original print, and even that, may have been anything but a close rendering of Peale.

The print by Valentine Green, declared to be from an original picture, presents another type, which, in comparison with the whole length by Wolff, a close copy as regards the figure and accessories, of a known original, warrants the assertion that the picture from which it is said to have been made, was not by Peale.

The print by Norman, an early American engraver, published in

3

1782, will be found copied as to the head, in the St. Aubin, the one published in the Universal Magazine, and possibly in that by Vinkeles. Dunlap in the appendix to his "History of the Arts of Design in the United States" mentions a whole length of Washington after C. W. Peale, as having been engraved by Robert Scott, an Englishman, who came to America about the year 1788, and settled in Philadelphia. No impression of this print, has come under the notice of the writer.

1. PEALE.

HIS EXCELL: G. WASHINGTON ESQ^r, LATE COMMANDER IN CHIEF OF THE ARMIES OF THE UNITED STATES OF AMERICA. Bust in uniform, Head to right. Oval, with border in a rectangle. *Mezzotinto.*

Height 7 8-16 inches; width 5 12-16 inches.

Painted & Engrav'd by C. W. Peale 1787.   *Very rare.*

There are three different states of this Plate:
1. Proof before all letters.
2. With the Title as above given, in the Border.
3. With the Title "His Excel. G: Washington Esq. L.L.D. Late Commander in Chief of the Armies of the U. S. of America & President of the Convention of 1787," in the Border.

2. ANDERSON.

GENERAL WASHINGTON. Bust in uniform, Head to right. Oval, with narrow border, in the upper part of a rectangle. The title in a ribbon beneath the oval.

Height 5 11-16 inches; width 3 6-16 inches.

[The American Spelling Book. By Noah Webster, Junr, Esquire. 14th Edition, N. Y. 1792.]

Cut on type metal by Alexander Anderson at seventeen years of age, when a student of medicine. Only one impression has come under the notice of the writer.

3. ANGUS.

GEN. WASHINGTON. Full Bust in uniform, Head to left, the right hand gloved, thrust in the breast. Circle, with border, upon a pyramidal Base, in a rectangle engraved to represent stone work. *Line.*

Height 5 13-16 inches; width 3 10-16 inches.

Wm Angus sc. *Published Sepr 23, 1785, by J. Fielding Pater Noster Row.*

[History of the War with America, France, Spain and Holland, commencing in 1775, and ending in 1783. By John Andrews, L.L.D. London, 1785.]

4. BUTTRE.

G. WASHINGTON. Three-quarter length, in the uniform of a Colonel in the Virginia Service. *Mixed.*

Height 4 13-16 inches; width 3 12-16 inches.

Painted by A. Dickinson. Engraved by J. C. Buttre.

[Recollections and Private Memoirs of Washington. By his adopted son George Washington Parke Custis. New York, 1860.]

5. CAREY.

GEN^L WASHINGTON. Bust in uniform, with black neckerchief, Head to left. Vignette. *Stipple.*

Height 2 4-16 inches; width 2 inches.

Carey Sc. (Printed in tint.)

Only one impression of this, has come under the notice of the writer.

6. CHEVILLET.

WASINGTON GÉNÉRALISSIME DES ETATS UNIS DE L'AMERIQUE. Full Bust in uniform, full face. Oval, with border in an ornamented rectangle. In the oval to the left a tree, the branches of which spread over and behind the head. The Title in a Tablet beneath the oval. *Line.*

Height 13 8-16 inches; width 10 inches.

Dessiné par Bounieu d'apres un Tableau fourni par M. le Marquis de la 'Fayette. Gravé par Chevillet. "Galérie des hommes Illustres vivans."
Rare.

An impression of this Plate, with the Title " Washington Généralissime des Americains, Libérateur des Etats Unis, contemporain et ami du General Lafayette," has come under the notice of the writer.

7. COOK.

GEORGE WASHINGTON. Bust in uniform, full face. Oval. *Line.*

Height 3 12-16 inches; width 3 inches.

T. Cook del et sculp. *Publish'd as the act directs Aug¹ 21ˢᵗ 1783 by S.* Bladon. *Rare in this State.*

Later impressions have the Title " Gen¹ Washington" and the address "Published by D. Brewman Oct¹ 1ˢᵗ 1792."

8. DE MARE.

WASHINGTON AT THE AGE OF TWENTY-FIVE. Bust in uniform. Head to right. Oval. *Line.*

Height 2 13-16 inches; width 2 5-16 inches.

J. De Mare. From a miniature on Ivory presented by Washington to his niece Harriet, and now belonging to her daughter's family. (Copy Right 1851.)

[Life of George Washington. By Washington Irving. New York 1856, '59.]

This is an error in the lettering. The miniature referred to, and from which the engraving was executed, was painted, according to a statement of Rembrandt Peale, in the year 1777, by his Father, Charles Willson Peale.

9. EDWIN.

GENERAL GEORGE WASHINGTON BORN FEB. 22. 1732 IN WEST-MORELAND COUNTY VIRGINIA, AND DIED DEC. 14. 1799 AT MOUNT VERNON. Full Bust, Head to left. *Stipple.*

Height 11 4-16 inches; width 9 inches.

R. Peale Pinx.   D. Edwin Sc.   *Rare.*

From the lettering of this Plate, it is usually considered to have been executed from
the first portrait by Rembrandt Peale, painted at the age of seventeen. But this, we
think, is an error, and if the engraving is a close rendering of its original, incline to
the opinion that the lettering is incorrect, and that it is really after one of Charles Willson Peale's later Portraits.

10. EDWIN.

GENERAL GEORGE WASHINGTON.   Full Bust, Head to left.

Stipple.

Height 12 15-16 inches; width 10 2-16 inches.

R. Peale Pinx^t.   D. Edwin Sculp^t.   Printed in Colours by H. Charles.
Published by H. S. Tanner Philadelphia.

The preceding print, with the addition of a border, which is included in the measure-
ment.

11. FORREST.

G. WASHINGTON 1772 Æt. 40.   Three quarter length, in the uniform
of a Colonel in the Virginia Service.   Vignette.   *Stipple.*

Height 5 4-16 inches; width 3 8-16 inches.

C. W. Peale.   J. B. Forrest.   Original in possession of G. W. P. Custis
Esq.   *New York, G. P. Putnam & Co.*

[Life of George Washington. By Washington Irving. New York
1856, '59.]

12. GREEN.

GENERAL WASHINGTON.   Full length in military costume, leaning
upon a Field piece to the left, a riding switch in his right hand.   The
left in which is his hat, rests upon a horse fore-shortened at the right.
In the extreme distance to left upon a hill, a large Building with cupola.

Mezzotinto.

Height 19 14-16 inches; width 14 inches.

Peel pinxit Philadelphia.   Stothard delin᷊ Londini.   J. Brown Excudit.
V. Green fecit mezzotinto Engraver to the king of Great Britain and the
Elector Palatine. *From an original Picture in the possession of Mr. Brown,*
Publish'd by him April 22ᵈ 1785, and sold at No. 10 *George Yard Lombard*
Street London.   *Extremely rare.*

Different from any other full length executed by Peale, and although ascribed to him
by the lettering of the print, and as having been painted at Philadelphia, its authenticity
is extremely doubtful.

13. HALDER.

Bust in uhiform, full face.   Oval of a single line.   (The etching of
the print by St. Aubin No 31)

Height 4 8-16 inches; width 4 inches.

Halder Sculp.

[Essai sur la Physiognomonie par Jean Gaspard Lavater.   Imprimé
à La Haye 1781–86.]

14. ——— ———.

LE GENERAL WASHINGTON Commendant En Chef Des Armées
Americaines né en Virginie en 1733. Bust in uniform, Head to right.
Oval, with border in a rectangle, resting upon a Tablet, in which is a
representation of the surrender at Yorktown, inscribed "Iournée mém-
orable du 19 Octobre 1781 à York en Virginie."   Title within the border.   *Line.*

Height 7 13-16 inches; width 5 8-16 inches.

Gravé d'apres le Tableau de N: Piehle peint d'apres nature à Philadelphie en 1783.   *Rare.*

[Essai sur la Physiognomonie par Jean Gaspard Lavater.   Imprimé à
La Haye 1781, '86.]

15. HOLLOWAY.

GENᴸ WASHINGTON.   Bust in uniform, Head to right.   Oval, with
border in a rectangle, beneath which is a representation of the surrender
at Yorktown, inscribed "Event of the 19ᵗʰ of Octʳ 1781 at Yorktown
in Virginia."   *Line.*

Height 7 11-16 inches; width 5 8-16 inches.

"The English artist has followed the lines of the print in the French original after a Picture by Piehle on account of the remarks of Mr. Lavater." T. Holloway Direxit. *Publish'd by T. Holloway & the other Proprietors, May* 21, 1794. *Rare.*

[Essays on Physiognomy. By John Caspar Lavater. Translated by Henry Hunter, D.D. London, 1789, '98.]

A copy of the preceding Print.

16. —— ——.

Bust in uniform, Head to right. Oval, with three lines for a narrow border, suspended by a Ring, above a Tablet containing a representation of the surrender at Yorktown. *Outline.*

Height 4 10-16 inches; width 3 12-16 inches.

Tom. 6 Pl. 339. *Extremely Rare.*

17. —— ——.

GENERAL WASHINGTON. Bust in uniform, Head to right. *Stipple.*

Height 3 4 16 inches; width 2 8-16 inches.

[Essays on Physiognomy. By The Rev. John Caspar Lavater. London, 1797.]

18. L.

S. E. GEORGE WASHINGTON Général en Chef des Armées des Etats Unis de l'Amerique. Full bust in uniform, full face, the right hand gloved, thrust in the breast. Oval, with border, resting upon a base in a rectangle. *Line.*

Height 10 5-16 inches; width 7 inches.

Le B. Pinx. J. L. Sculp.

19. LE BEAU.

GEORGES WASHINGTON EQ^{er} Général en Chef de l'Armée Anglo-Ameriquaine nomé Dictateur par le Congrès en Fevrier 1777. Full Bust in uniform and Cocked Hat, Head to left, a drawn sword partly seen on the left. Oval, with border in a rectangle, resting upon a Base, the Title in a Tablet upon the Base. *Line.*

Height 6 4-16 inches; width 4 8-16 inches.

Desrais del.   Le Beau sculp.   *A Paris chez Esnauts et Rapilly, rue St Jacques à la ville de Coutances.* *Rare.*

This appears to be a combination of the Peale, and the one known as the Campbell Portrait.

20. LE BEAU.

S. E. GEORGE WASHINGTON, Général en Chef des Armées des Etats-Unis de l'Amerique. Full Bust in uniform, Head to right. Oval, with border upon a Base in an ornamental rectangle, at the top of the oval, the word "Libertas" in three lines, surrounded by rays; beneath the oval, war emblems. *Line.*

Height 6 10-16 inches; width 4 8-16 inches.

Le Beau sculp.   *A Paris chez Mondhare rue St Jacques.* *Extremely rare.*

21. LE MIRE.

LE GENERAL WASHINGTON, ne Quid Detrimenti Capiat Res publica. Full length in uniform, standing to the left in front of a tent, in his right hand, a roll displaying sheets inscribed "Declaration of Independence," "Treaty of Alliance &c". His left hand gloved, is thrust into the breast. Beneath his feet are various torn documents, marked "Protection to Rebels," "Conciliatory Bills &c &c". In the rear a negro servant with a horse, and in the extreme right distance, on lower ground an encampment. *Line.*

Height 16 10-16 inches; width 12 11-16 inches.

Peint par L. le Paon Peintre de Bataille de S. A. S. M. le Prince de Condé. Gravé par N. le Mire des Academies Imperiales et Royales et de celle des sciences et arts de Rouen (1780). Gravé d'apres le Tableau original appartenant a Mr. Marquis de la Fayette. *Cette Estampe ce vend avec Privilege du Roy a Paris chez le Mire Graveur rue et porte St Jacques Maison de M^r le Camus M^d de Drap, prix 12 livres.*

Engraved from a fictitious picture, the head alone after Peale. Le Paon also painted a full length of Lafayette, which Le Mire engraved as a companion print to the Washington.

22. —— ——.

GENERAL WASHINGTON. Full figure in uniform, standing to the left, in front of a tent. *Mezzotinto.*

Height 12 14-16 inches; width 9 14-16 inches.

Printed for and sold by Carington Bowles N° 69 in St Paul's Church Yard London. Published as the act directs 24 June 1785.
Extremely rare.

A copy of the preceding Print, omitting the tree in the rear of the Tent, and the Landscape to the right.

23. —— ——.

GENERAL WASHINGTON LATE PRESIDENT OF THE UNITED STATES OF AMERICA. Full figure in uniform, standing to the left, in an easy attitude in front of a Tent, in the right hand an open scroll, inscribed "Declaration of American Independence." The left hand gloved, is thrust into the breast. In the left foreground a camp stool, upon which is a field glass and cocked Hat, and in the right distance on lower ground, the view of an encampment. *Mezzotinto.*

Height 13 5-16 inches; width 10 inches.

Published 25th May 1797 by Laurie & Whittle 53 Fleet Street London.
Extremely rare.

A copy of No. 21 with the variations noted.

4

24. —— ——.

GEORGE WASHINGTON ESQUIER, General et Comandeur en Chef d'Armée des XIII Provinces unies en Amerique. Half length in uniform, Head to left, the right hand thrust in the breast. Oval in a rectangle.   *Mezzotinto.*

Height 7 15-16 inches; width 6 4-16 inches.

Se vend a Londres chez Thom. Hart.   *Extremely rare.*

25. NEWTON.

GEN^L WASHINGTON. Bust in uniform, with black neckerchief, Head to right. Vignette.   *Stipple.*

Height 2 4-16 inches; width 2 inches.

Jas. Newton sculp. (Printed in Tint.)   *Extremely rare.*

26. NORMAN.

HIS EXCELL^Y GEORGE WASHINGTON ESQ^R General and Commander in Chief of the Allied Armiés supporting the Independence of America. Bust in uniform, full face. Oval, with border in a rectangle, resting upon a small pedestal, inscribed Temperance, Prudence, Fortitude, Justice. Emblems of war on either side.   *Line.*

Height 11 7-16 inches; width 9 3-16 inches.

B. Blyth del. J. Norman sculp. Taken from an original Picture in possession of his Ex^cy Gov. Hancock. *Published by John Coles, Boston March 26th 1782.*

Only one impression of this, has come to the knowledge of the writer. It is the first engraved Portrait of Washington, executed by a professional engraver in America. The Mezzotinto by Peale, referred to in the text, as advertised for sale in 1780, although the first in point of time, must be considered in a different light, as Peale was not a professional engraver, the few plates he produced, six in number, being after his own designs.

27. PARADISE.

WASHINGTON Æt. 40. Three quarter length, in the uniform of a colonel in the Virginia Service. Landscape background. *Line.*

Height 4 11-16 inches: width 3 13-16 inches.

Engraved by J. W. Paradise From a Picture by J. W. Chapman after C. W. Peale. From the original Portrait in the possession of G. W. P. Custis Esqr Arlington House.

[The writings of George Washington. By Jared Sparks, Boston, 1834.]

28. PARKER.

G. WASHINGTON 1772 Æt. 40. Three quarter length, in the uniform of a colonel in the Virginia Service. Vignette. *Stipple.*

Height 4 12-16 inches; width 3 12-16 inches.

C. W. Peale. Geo. Parker. Original in possession of G. W. P. Custis Esqr. Arlington House. *New York G. P. Putnam & Co.*

[Life of George Washington. By Washington Irving. New York, 1855. 8vo. Ed.]

29. PRUNEAU.

GEORGE WASHINGTON COMMANDANT EN CHEF DES ARMÉES DES ETATS-UNIS DE L'AMERIQUE. Bust in uniform, with black neckerchief. Head to right. Oval, with narrow border (in a rectangle) resting upon a Base, upon which is the Title. Over the oval, a rattle-snake and Liberty cap. *Line.*

Height 6 2-16 inches; width 4 4-16 inches.

N. Pruneau del. et sculp. *A Paris chez l'auteur rue St. Jacques vis à vis le college du Plessis et chez Dennel graveur rue du P^x Bourbon atten^t la Foire St Germain. Extremely rare.*

A copy in reverse of the print by William Sharp No. 35 the legend in the upper border "Don't Tread on me," omitted.

30. ROGERS.

G. WASHINGTON. Three quarter length, in the uniform of a colonel in the Virginia Service. Oval, with ornamental border. Landscape background. *Line.*

Height 6 inches; width 5 inches.

C. W. Peale. J. Rogers. *New York Virtue Emmons & Co.*

[The Life of George Washington. By Benson J. Lossing. New York, 1860.]

31. ST. AUBIN.

GEORGE WASHINGTON COMMANDANT EN CHEF DES ARMÉES AMERICAINES, NÉ EN VIRGINIE EN 1733. Bust in uniform, full face. Oval medallion, in a rectangle; beneath the oval, a Tablet in which is the Title. *Line.*

Height 7 12-16 inches; width 5 10-16 inches.

Se trouve à Paris, chez Aug. De St Aubin, Graveur du Roi, et de sa Bibliotheque, actuellement rue Therese Bute St Roch et a la Bibliotheque du Roi et chez Mr Cochin, aux Galleries du Louvre A. P. D. R.

Rare.

32. —— ——.

WASHINGTON. Full Bust in uniform, Head to right. *Outline.*

Height 3 6-16 inches; width 2 3-16 inches.

N. Piehle pinx^t. Landon direx^t. "Hist. D'Amerique."

33. SANDS.

WASHINGTON. Full Bust in uniform, Head to left. *Outline.*

Height 4 inches; width 2 9-16 inches.

R. Sands sculp. *Published by Vernor Hood & Sharpe Poultry Jan^y* 1, 1811.

[The Historic Gallery of Portraits and Paintings and Biographical Review. London, 1807-11.]

A copy in reverse of the preceding print.

34. SARTAIN.

HIS EXCEL. G: WASHINGTON ESQ: L.L.D. Late Commander in Chief of the Armies of the U. S. of America & President of the Convention of 1787. Bust in uniform, Head to right. Oval, with border in a rectangle; the Title in the Border.   *Mezzotinto.*

Height 6 inches; width 4 12-16 inches.

Engraved by John Sartain from the original print in possession of W. A. Whiteman Esqr. engraved by C. W. Peale in 1787 from a painting by himself.

[Andreana.   Horace W. Smith, Philadelphia, 1865.]

A copy of the mezzotinto by Peale, No. 1.   Later impressions are without the Border or rectangle, both having been removed.   They are without Title, the oval 4 3-16 inches in height by 3 6-16 inches in width.   Some are printed in Tint.

35. SHARP.

GEORGE WASHINGTON Commander en Chief of ÿ Armies of ÿ United States of America. Bust in uniform, with black neckerchief, Head to left. Oval, with border in a rectangle, above a Tablet in which is the Title; over the oval, a rattle snake and Liberty cap, with the legend "Don't Tread on me." At the sides, olive and laurel branches, Flags &c. On the Flag to the right thirteen Stars.   *Line.*

Height 6 3-16 inches; width 4 7-16 inches.

Engrav'd by W. Sharp from an original Picture. *London Published according to act of Parliament Feb^r 22^d 1780.   Rare in this State.*

[A Poetical Epistle to his Excellency George Washington Esquire, Commander in Chief of the Armies of the United States of America, From an Inhabitant of the State of Maryland, to which is annexed a short sketch of General Washington's Life and Character.   Annapolis 1779 London Re-printed 1780.]

Subsequently prefixed to "The Constitutions of the several Independent States of America &c, By the Rev. William Jackson London 1783," the date in the address altered to 1783, and with the addition, "by J. Stockdale Piccadilly." Although this is declared to have been engraved from an original Picture, certain allusions made to it at the time, which may be found in Doane's memoir of the author of the Epistle, the Rev. Charles Henry Wharton D.D. (Philadelphia 1834), would seem to indicate, that the picture was made up from a print, "front face Bust size," obtained from Paris, and that Benjamin West, who had been applied to for that purpose, may have executed it for the purpose of the engraver.

36. STEEL.

WASHINGTON IN 1772 ÆTATIS 40. Three quarter length, in the uniform of a Colonel in the Virginia Service.   *Line.*

Height 5 9-16 inches; width 4 5-16 inches.

Painted by A. Dickinson. Engraved by J. W. Steel. "I certify that the painting of Washington in 1772, executed by Anson Dickinson Esq. from the original picture by Peale in my possession, is a faithful resemblance of the original, the only original of the Pater Patriæ prior to the Revolution. Arlington House July 18, 1830. George W. P. Custis." *Entered according to act of Congress* 1833 *by A. Dickinson &c.*

37. TRENCHARD.

GENERAL WASHINGTON. Bust in uniform, Head to right. Oval, with border in a rectangle, engraved to represent stone work. Beneath the oval, a Tablet and the Washington arms, with the motto, "Exitus Acta Probat."   *Line.*

Height 6 inches; width 3 10-16 inches.

J. Trenchard Sc^pt.

[Columbian Magazine. Philadelphia January 1787.]

This appears to be a combination of the Peale and Pine Portraits, probably a make up of the engraver.

38. TRENCHARD.

HIS EXCEL: G: WASHINGTON ESQ. Bust in uniform, Head to right. Oval, with narrow border, resting upon a Base in a rectangle. Title in the Base. A Laurel wreath and branches, at top of oval.

Line.

Height 6 4-16 inches; width 3 14-16 inches.

[The American Spelling Book, In three parts. By Noah Webster Jun. Esq. 12th Edition. Philadelphia 1789.]

A copy of the mezzotinto by Peale No. 1. Only one impression has come under the notice of the writer, it shows considerable wear of the Plate.

39. VINKELES.

G. WASHINGTON GENERAL DER NOORD-AMERICAANEN. Bust in uniform, Head to left. Inclosed with a border, resembling a picture frame suspended over a Pedestal (in a rectangle), upon which lies a Hat, baton &c. A curtain hangs over and conceals the upper left corner of the Frame.

Line.

Height 5 10-16 inches; width 3 8-16 inches.

Rein' Vinkeles sculp. naar een origineel Schildery by den Wel Ed. Heer P. Van Winter Nic: Z.

40. WOLFF.

WASHINGTON (GEORGES) PRESIDENT DE LA REPUBLIQUE DES ETATS-UNIS D'AMERIQUE DU NORD X 1799. Full length in uniform, standing to the right, leaning by the left hand upon a Field piece. In the rear, an attendant with a horse and a flag partly shown, upon which, in a circle thirteen stars. In the left distance, a Building with cupola (Nassau Hall, Princeton), with some Troops in the middle ground. *Mixed.*

Height 9 11-16 inches; width 6 6-16 inches.

Tableau du temps. Gravé par Wolff. Dessiné par Girardet. "Gal^rie hist^que de Versailles." (Paris 1838.)

A close rendering of the picture commenced at Valley Forge referred to in the text, with the exception of the head, the character of which has not been preserved.

41. ZERLAMSLER.

WASHINGTON. Bust in uniform, Head to right. Title in border.
Outline.

Height 4 4-16 inches; width 2 10-16 inches.

Zerlamsler sc.

Only one impression of this, has come under the notice of the writer.

42. —— ——.

GEN.ᴸ WASHINGTON. Bust in uniform with black neckerchief, Head
to right. Vignette.   *Stipple.*

Height 4 6-16 inches; width 3 10-16 inches.

Published Noͬ 1ˢᵗ 1784 by Whitworth & Yates Bradford Street.

Only one impression of this, has come under the notice of the writer.

43. —— ——.

GEORGE WASHINGTON Commander in chief of the American
Army. Bust in uniform, full face. Oval, with border upon a Base, in
a rectangle.   *Line.*

Height 5 11-16 inches; width 3 6-16 inches.

Engraved for the Universal Magazine. *Printed for J. Hinton at the
Kings Arms in Paternoster Row.*

44. —— ——.

GENERAL WASHINGTON. Bust in uniform, Head slightly to left.
Oval. *Stipple.*   *Rare.*

Height 3 12-16 inches; width 3 1-16 inches.

45. —— ——.

EL GENERAL VVASHINGTON. Bust in uniform, Head slightly to
right. Circle, with border the sides partly reduced, in a square. *Line.*

Height 4 11 16 inches; width 4 6-16 inches.

Only one impression of this, has come under the notice of the writer. A Spanish
engraving.

ALEXANDER CAMPBELL.

1775.

ALTHOUGH the references on some of the prints in the appended list, claim the originals to have been "drawn from the Life by Alexander Campbell of Williamsburg in Virginia," yet in every sense they may be classed among the Fictitious Portraits. There is no record of any such painter or draughtsman, and Washington himself declared that he never saw Mr. Campbell. The presumption is that the portrait or portraits, for according to the prints there appear to have been two, one mounted, the other a three-quarter length (Nos. 46 and 49 in the list), and to which all bear more or less of a resemblance, were manufactured at the beginning of the revolutionary war, for some enterprising publisher either in London or on the Continent, for the express purpose of being engraved, in anticipation of a demand which it was felt must arise. Portraits of Gates, Putnam, Charles Lee, Sullivan, and other officers of the army, were published at the same time, forming sets, and apparently executed by the same engravers, with no better claim to authenticity.

They have, however, not been placed among the Fictitious, as they seem to have a distinct type of themselves, and are well known to the curious collector, the date of publication 1775 on the two mentioned above, assigning them to this chronological order. As only four of these prints bear the name of the engraver, the alphabetical arrangement has, in this case, been in a measure dispensed with, those which

5   (33)

seem to have the closest resemblance, being consecutive. Very few of them possess much artistic merit; that published at Paris by " Esnauts et Rapilly," engraver unknown, being one of the best.

46. ——— ———.

GEORGE WASHINGTON ESQ^R General and Commander in chief of the Continental Army in America. Full figure in uniform and cocked Hat, on horseback, advancing to the right. A drawn sword in the right hand, is held across the body. A Battle in the right distance.

Mezzotinto.

Height 12 8-16 inches; width 9 14-16 inches.

Done from an original Drawn from the Life by Alex^r Campbell of Williamsburgh in Virginia. *Published as the act directs 9 Septr 1775 by C. Shepherd.* *Very rare.*

This is the print, an impression of which Joseph Reed presented to Mrs. Washington, and referred to by Washington, in his letter to Reed, dated Cambridge 31st Jany. 1776. " Mrs. Washington desires I will thank you for the picture sent her. Mr. Campbell, whom I never saw to my knowledge, has made a very formidable figure of the Commander-in-chief, giving him a sufficient portion of terror in his countenance."

47. NILSON.

GEORGE WASHINGTON ESQ^R General and Commander in chief of the Continental Army in America. Full figure in uniform and cocked Hat, on horseback advancing to the right, a drawn sword in right hand. In the back ground, on the horizon, the upper portions of a large fortification extend across the print. Inclosed by a narrow square border. *Line.*

Height 7 inches; width 5 10-16 inches.

Nach dem Leben gezeichnet von Alexander Champbele von Williamsburg in Virginien. *Nilson fec. et excud A. V.* *Extremely rare.*

The same figure as in the preceding print. The horse however is entirely different, having a short tail, trappings the same.

48. —— ——.

GEORGE WASHINGTON ESQ^R AMERICANISCHER GENERALISSIMUS. Three quarter length, in uniform and cocked Hat, with a drawn sword in right hand. Oval, with border only partly showing at the sides. *Etched.*   *Rare.*

Height 6 4-16 inches; width 3 10-16 inches.

49. —— ——.

GEORGE WASHINGTON ESQ^R GENERAL AND COMMANDER IN CHIEF OF THE CONTINENTAL ARMY IN AMERICA. Three quarter length in uniform and cocked Hat, pointing to a Battle in left distance, the left hand on his hip. The head is turned to the right, the body to the left.

Mezzotinto.

Height 12 13-16 inches; width 9 5-16 inches.

Done from an original Drawn from the Life of Alex^r Campbell of Williamsburg in Virginia. *Published as the act directs 9 Sept.* 1775 *by* C. *Shepherd London.*   *Rare.*

A later state of the Plate, in which there are some slight variations bears the address " Ioh Martin Will excud. Aug. Vind."

50. —— ——.

GEORGE WASHINGTON EQUIER GENERAL ET COMENDEUR EN CHIEF D'ARMÉE DE XIII PROVINCES UNIS EN AMERIQUE. Full Bust, in uniform and cocked Hat, head three quarters to right. Oval, in a rectangle.

Mezzotinto.

Height 8 inches; width 6 2-16 inches.

peint par Alexander Campbell à Williamsburg en Virginie. *Se vend* à *Londres chez Thom. Hart.*   *Very rare.*

51. —— ——.

GEORG WASHINGTON ESQ^R. COMMANDIRENDER GENERAL EN CHIEF DER PROVINZIAL-ARMÉE IN NORD AMERIKA. Nearly half-length, in uniform and cocked Hat, head three quarters to right, body slightly to left. Oval, with border in a rectangle resting upon a Base, in which is the Title. *Line.*   *Rare.*

Height 6 inches: width 3 8-16 inches.

52. —— ——.

WASHINGTON General dans l'Armée des Americains. Three quarter length, in uniform and cocked Hat, pointing to a Battle in the right distance, the right hand upon the hip. Body to right, Head three quarter to left. *Etched.* *Very rare.*

Height 6 8-16 inches; width 5 2-16 inches.

A copy in reverse with some variations in the Landscape and clouds of No. 49.

53. FRITZSCH.

GEORG WASHINGTON ESQ[R] Commandirender General en chef der Provinzialarmée in Nordamerika. Full Bust, in uniform and cocked Hat, body to left, head three quarters to right. Oval, with border resting upon a Base. The Title on a Tablet, in the Base.

Line.

Height 6 inches; width 3 8-16 inches.

T. C. G. Fritzsch sc. *Extremely rare.*

54. —— ——.

GEN[L] GEORGE WASHINGTON. Full Bust in uniform, Head to right. Oval, with square border upon a Base, in a rectangle engraved to represent stone work. A wreath tied by a ribbon, extends from the top of the border, down each side. *Line.*

Height 5 9-16 inches; width 3 7-16 inches.

[The History of America from the first Discovery by Columbus to the conclusion of the late war. By William Russel, LL.D. London, 1779.]

55. LIEBE.

GEN[L] GEORGE WASHINGTON. Full Bust in uniform, Head to left.

Line.

Height 5 12-16 inches; width 3 8-16 inches.

Liebe Sc. (*The Reverse of the preceding print.*) *Rare.*

56. —— ——.

GENERAL WASHINGTON. Bust, in uniform and cocked Hat, head three quarters to left. Oval, with border engraved to represent stone work. *Line.*

Height 4 4-16 inches; width 3 6-16 inches.

Engraved for Murray's History of the American War. *Printed for T. Robson Newcastle upon Tyne.* (London 1782.)

57. RUGENDAS.

GEORGE WASHINGTON ESQ^R GENERAL AND COMMANDER IN CHEF OF THE CONTINENTAL ARMY IN AMERICA. Three quarter length, in uniform and cocked Hat, a drawn sword in the right hand, the arm across the body. Head slightly to left, Body to right. On the left, the muzzle of a large cannon (discharging), and to the right some shipping. *Mezzotinto.*

Height 11 13-16 inches; width 8 14-16 inches.

Joh. Lorenz Rugendas sculpsit et excud. Aug. Vind. *Very rare.*

Another State of the Plate, with the Title in different letters, has the word "Chief," instead of "Chef."

58. —— ——.

GEORGE WASHINGTON EQ^{RR} GÈNÈRAL EN CHEF DE L'ARMÉE ANGLO-AMERIQUAINE, NOMMÉ DICTATEUR PAR LE CONGRÈS EN FEVRIER 1777. Full Bust, in uniform and cocked Hat, a drawn sword partly visible on the left. Oval, with border in a rectangle, ornamented with war Emblems &c. *Line.*

Height 6 4-16 inches; width 4 8-16 inches,

A Paris chez Esnauts et Rapilly, rue St Jacques à la Ville de Coutances, A.P.D.R. · *Rare.*

59. —— ——.

GEORGE WASHINGTON EQ^{RR} GÈNÈRAL EN CHEF DE L'ARMÈE ENGLO AMERIQUAINE NOMMÉ DICTATEUR PAR LE CONGRÈS EN FEVRIER 1777. GEORGE WASHINGTON EQ^{ER} GENERAL AND COMMANDER EN CHIEF

OF THE CONTINENTAL ARMY IN AMERICA. Half length, in uniform and cocked Hat, head to left. A drawn sword in the right hand, is held across the body. The Titles in a Tablet, in the lower border. *Line.*

Height 11 12-16 inches; width 7 5-16 inches.

d'apres l'original de Champell Peintre de Williamsbourg capitale de la Virginie. *Extremely rare.*

60. —— ——.

GEORG WASHINGTON ESQ^R. Half length, in uniform and cocked Hat, body to right, head to left. Oval, with border resting upon a base in a rectangle. Title on the Base. *Etched.*   *Rare.*

Height 4 8-16 inches; width 2 13-16 inches. .

61. —— ——.

GEORG^R WASHINGTON GENERAL UND COMANDEUR EN CHEF BEY DER PROVINCIAL-ARMÈE IN AMERICA. Three quarter length, in uniform and cocked Hat, head three quarters to right, body slightly to left. The right hand is extended, and the left upon the hip. In the left distance, a Battle. *Etched.*   *Rare.*

Height 5 10-16 inches; width 3 5-16 inches.

62. —— ——.

GENERAL WASHINGTON. Full figure, in uniform and cocked Hat, on horseback, advancing to the right. A drawn sword in right hand, head turned to the left. The horse is rearing. In the landscape, a stream of water to the right. *Line.*

Height 5 12-16 inches; width 4 inches.

Very rare.

PIERRE EUGENE DU SIMITIERE.

1779.

Portrait painter and designer, was born at Geneva in the first quarter of the eighteenth century, and after spending about ten years in the West Indies, travelling from island to island, practicing his art and collecting shells and botanical specimens, finally settled in Philadelphia in the early part of 1766.

Du Simitière was a man of considerable ingenuity, an active member and one of the officers of the "American Philosophical Society," and formed a Cabinet of Natural History, the "American Museum," which the Marquis de Chastellux visited when in Philadelphia, December, 1780, and speaks of as being greatly celebrated, and unrivalled in America. He also made a large collection of cotemporary historical matter, which is now in the possession of the Philadelphia Library Company. Pierre Eugène Du Simitière died at Philadelphia, October, 1784.

The earliest dated print in the appended list, published at Madrid in 1781, is inscribed as having been executed from an original drawn from life at Philadelphia, and the same statement is made on the one by Prevost, and on each of the set of thirteen profile portraits including a Washington, engraved by Reading and published at London in 1783. Beyond this, there appears to be no evidence that Washington sat to Du Simitière for this portrait, the first profile of him of which we have any knowledge, but the presumption is altogether in

(39)

favor of the fact. The artist's recognised position in the community, would certainly obtain for him such a privilege, and it seems scarcely probable that a student of history and lover of nature, such as we know Du Simitière to have been, would think for a moment of manufacturing likenesses of the distinguished men of the day, and let them go out as if from life.

The year 1779 is given as the probable chronology, Washington having passed the greater part of the winter of 1778–79 in Philadelphia.

The profile by Du Simitière which is known to us only through the art of engraving, represents Washington in a military coat, with his hair carefully dressed and tied by a ribbon into a queue, and there is reason to suppose that it and the others included in the set above mentioned, were merely water color drawings neatly executed for the purpose of the engraver, and then, perhaps, laid aside and forgotten. While it may not strictly be termed an ordinary head, yet it reveals no particular force or ability, and represents rather a well-bred, courteous gentleman, neat in person, and mindful of all the amenities of life, an officer probably, but not a commander.

With the exception of the one by Ruotte, in which a little more firmness and decision is given to the head, nearly all the prints in the list, that by Brandi being most probably the prototype, bear a close resemblance to each other, and are well engraved.

63. ADAM.

WASHINGTON. Bust in uniform, Head in profile to left.   Circular medallion, suspended by a ring, over a Base in a rectangle.   *Line.*

Height 5 2-16 inches; width 3 8-16 inches.

Dessinò d'aprùs Nature par Du Simitier a Philadelphie.   Gravò par Adam.

[Complot D'Arnold et De Sir Henry Clinton Contre Les Etats-Unis D'Amerique et contre Le Général Washington, Septembre 1780.   Paris 1816.]

64. BRANDI.

EL GENERAL WASHINGTON.   Bust in uniform, in profile to left. Circular medallion, suspended by a ring, and resting upon a Base in a rectangle.   The Title upon the Base.

Height 4 14·16 inches; width 3 6·16 inches.

Sacado del natural por Mʳ Du Simitier en Filadelfia. Grabado por Mariano Brandi en Madrid à·1781.

Only one impression of this, has come under the notice of the writer.

65. E.

HIS EXCELLENCY GENERAL WASHINGTON Commander in Chief of the United States of North America &c.   Full Bust in uniform, Head in profile to right.   Oval, in a rectangle.   *Line.*

Height 4 8·16 inches; width 3 10·16 inches.

B. B. E.   *Pubᵈ May 15ᵗʰ 1783 by R. Wilkinson Nᵒ 58 Cornhill London.*   *Rare in early state.*

[Heads of Illustrious Americans and others, number 1.   Containing Portraits of General Washington, Henry Laurens Esq. John Jay Esq. S. Huntingdon Esq. Charles Thompson Esq. J. Dickinson Esq. Silas Deane Esq. General Read, Governeer Morris Esq. Maj. Gen. Baron Steuben, W. H. Drayton Esq. Maj. Gen. Gates.]

66. KUFFNER.

G. WASHINGTON.   Bust in uniform, Head in profile to left.   Oval.
                                                        Stipple.
Height 3 2·16 inches; width 2 10·16 inches.

A. W. Kuffner sc. 1793.   *Rare.*

6

67. PREVOST.

G. WASHINGTON. Bust in uniform, Head in profile to left.   Circular medallion, suspended by a ring, over a Base in a rectangle.   *Line.*

Height 4 15-16 inches; width 3 7-16 inches.

Drawn from the life by Du Simetiere in Philadelphia.   Engraved by B. L. Prevost at Paria.

68. READING.

GENERAL WASHINGTON. Bust in uniform, Head in profile to right. Oval.   *Stipple.*

Height 2 14-16 inches; width 2 7-16 inches.

B. Reading sculpt.   Drawn from the Life by Du Simetiere in Philadelphia.   *Publish'd May* 10*th* 1783 *by* W*m* *Richardson N°* 174 *Strand.* (Also printed in Tint.)

[Thirteen Portraits of American Legislators, Patriots and Soldiers, who distinguished themselves in rendering their country independent, viz. General Washington, General Baron De Steuben, Silas Deane, General Reed, Governor Morris, General Gates, John Jay, W. H. Drayton, Henry Laurens, Charles Thompson, S. Huntingdon, J. Dickenson, General Arnold.   Drawn from the Life By Du Simitiere, Painter and member of the Philosophical Society in Philadelphia.   London n. d.]

69. RUOTTE.

G. WASHINGTON né en Virginie Année 1733 Commendant en chef des Armées et Président du Congrès d'Amerique.   Full Bust in uniform, Head in profile to left.   Oval.   *Stipple.*

Height 4 2-16 inches; width 3 5-16 inches.

F. Bonneville deli.   Ruotte sculp.   *Paris Rue S*t *Jacques N°* 195.

70. ———— ——.

GENt WASHINGTON. Bust in uniform, Head in profile to left.   Oval, with border upon a Base, in a rectangle.   *Line.*

Height 5 9-16 inches; width 3 8-16 inches.

Publish'd Jan 31, 1784 *by John Walker from an original Painting.*
                                                            Rare.

71. —— ——.

WASHINGTON.   Full Bust in uniform, Head in profile to right.   Vignette.   *Line.*

Height 2 inches.

72. —— ——.

GEORG WASHINGTON.   Bust in uniform, profile to right.   Circular
medallion, upon a Base in a rectangle.   The Title upon the Base.
                                                          Etched.

Height 4 8-16 inches; width 3 inches.

WILLIAM DUNLAP.

1783.

PAINTER and author, was born at Perth Amboy, February 19, 1766. The family removed to New York in the spring of 1777, and without much previous instruction other than that derived from copying prints, and the observation of the few pictures accessible to him at the time, he commenced drawing portraits in crayon, when about sixteen years of age.

In the autumn of 1783, while visiting Mr. John Van Horne, who resided within a short distance of Washington's head-quarters at Rocky Hill, near Princeton, New Jersey, he drew the portraits of his host and hostess. These having been seen by the General, who frequently called at the house, and receiving his approbation, Mr. Van Horne requested him to sit to the young artist, to which he complied. Dunlap in his autobiography refers to it in the following manner: "This was a triumphant moment for a boy of seventeen; and it must be remembered that Washington had not then been 'hackneyed to the touches of painter's pencil;' I say a triumphant moment, but it was one of anxiety, fear, and trembling." He visited head-quarters frequently, also drawing the portrait of Mrs. Washington, and after taking copies for himself, presented the originals to Mr. and Mrs. Van Horne.

In the following year, Dunlap went to London to study painting under Benjamin West, remaining four years, and after his return, led a varied career, alternating through a long life between business, the

(44)

studio, the stage, and literature. He wrote several plays (and appeared once upon the stage himself), a life of Brockden Brown, one of Cooke, a history of New Netherlands, and one of the American Theatre. He executed several large pictures, painted many portraits, travelling constantly for the purpose, and took an active part in establishing the "National Academy of Design," New York.

In old age, and under reduced circumstances, he compiled the "History of the rise and progress of the Arts of Design in the United States," which was published in 1834. William Dunlap died in New York, September 28, 1839.

We have but one engraving after this drawing, which, if not a fine example of mezzotinto, may be a good rendering of the original.

73. ROBIN.

GEORGE WASHINGTON. Full Bust in uniform, Head three quarters to right. *Mezzotinto.*

Height 3 12-16 inches; width 2 6-16 inches.

From the original picture in Pastel Painted from life by William Dunlap, and now (1868) in the possession of Dr. Samuel C. Ellis New York. *Elias Dexter 564 Broadway New York.*

JOSEPH WRIGHT.

1783–1790.

Son of Joseph Wright and Patience Lovell, was born at Borden-town, New Jersey, July 16, 1756. After the death of his father, his mother went with her family of three children to London, where, becoming famous for modelling in wax, she was enabled to give her son a good education. Turning his attention to portrait painting, he received advice and instruction from Benjamin West and John Hopp-ner, who married his sister, and previous to leaving England, had painted the portrait of the Prince of Wales, afterwards George the Fourth.

In the early part of 1782, being placed under the protection of Ben-jamin Franklin, he went to Paris for the purpose of prosecuting his studies in the art. He, however, remained but a short time, and being provided with letters from Franklin to General Washington, set sail in October of that year for the United States, which he reached after a perilous voyage of ten weeks, landing at Boston.

In the autumn of the following year, 1783, he painted the portrait of Washington, at his head-quarters, Rocky Hill, near Princeton, N. J., for which he had several sittings. A portrait of Washington, in pos-session of Mrs. Annie Hopkinson Foggo, of Philadelphia, a great-grand-daughter of Francis Hopkinson, is by Wright. It is a full bust, in Continental uniform, full face, the body turned to the left, the hair short and undressed. The pose is awkward, and while having no pretensions to artistic merit, conveys the impression of at least an ear-

(46)

nest attempt on the part of the painter to reproduce that which was before him. It is in good preservation, painted on a mahogany panel 14 by 11 inches. This picture was owned by Francis Hopkinson, and has never been out of the family, and there is reason to suppose that it may be the one painted at Rocky Hill above mentioned. The print by O'Neill, No. 93, bears a slight resemblance to it.

In the winter of 1783-4, Wright, then in Philadelphia, painted another portrait of Washington, which, it appears by the following letter to him from the General, was intended as a present to Count de Solms. " Mt. Vernon, 10th Jan. 1784. Sir: When you have finished my portrait which is intended for the Count de Solms, I will thank you for handing it to Mr. Robert Morris, who will forward it to the Count de Bruhl (Minister from his Electoral Highness of Saxe at the Court of London), as the channel pointed out for the conveyance of it. As the Count de Solms proposes to honour it with a place in his collection of military characters, I am persuaded you will not be deficient in point of execution. Be so good as to forward the cost of it to me, and I will remit the money. Let it (after Mr. Morris has seen it) be carefully packed to prevent injury."

An authentic portrait by Wright, which was painted in Philadelphia for Mrs. Elizabeth Powel of that city, is now in the possession of her great-nephew, Mr. Samuel Powel, of Newport, R. I. It is a half-length, in uniform, life size, the right hand resting upon a sword, full face, the body turned to the right; signed and dated "J. Wright, 1784." Tuckerman, in referring to it in his work on "The Character and Portraits of Washington," says: "Perhaps no portrait of Washington bears such convincing marks of genuine individuality, without a particle of artistic flattery." This picture has not been engraved.

After Washington was inaugurated President, Wright was desirous of procuring another sitting, which was refused in consequence of the exacting cares and duties of the office. The artist, however, was determined on his purpose, and the President being a regular attendant at St. Paul's Chapel, Broadway, New York, where a canopied pew had been prepared for his reception, Wright obtained permission of the occupant of the one immediately opposite, to use that position for a Sunday morning or two to take a deliberate miniature profile likeness of him in crayon, as he sat entirely unconscious of the act. This he afterwards etched himself, with considerable taste and excellence of execution, and published it printed on a card. It is a profile bust in uniform, with the hair dressed and tied by a ribbon into a queue, and is well drawn; there is a quiet dignity about the head which is quite impressive, and it is altogether, an exceedingly interesting production. It seems to have been an accepted likeness, judging from the number of contemporary copies of it, and the certificate to that effect on the impression owned by Elkanah Watson, referred to below. This is the first print mentioned in the appended List.

Wright took a plaster cast of Washington's features at Mount Vernon in 1784, from which he seems to have modelled a bust, and from this, perhaps, those of his mother's in wax, which are well known, may have been taken. A wax bas-relief portrait of Washington in the possession of Benjamin R. Smith, of Philadelphia, executed by Wright for Thomas Richardson, of Newport, and which bears his name, in which the head is laureated, is quite striking and characteristic.

Upon the establishment of the Mint at Philadelphia, Wright was appointed draughtsman and die-sinker thereto, and it is probable that the first coins and medals executed in this country were his handiwork.

The Washington medal known as the "Manly Medal," published at Philadelphia in 1790, is supposed to be by him. Wright died shortly after his appointment, being carried off by the yellow fever of the year 1793.

Besides the original etching, and the copies of it more or less close, there will be found in the appended list two other and different types of portraits, both in uniform, one in full profile as engraved by Holloway, Murray, and Roosing, and the other in which the bust is in three-quarters, and the face in profile, engraved by Evans, Scoles, and others. We are unable to say from what pictures these were taken. The print by Evans, however, ascribes it to be after a drawing by Wright, while that by Holloway gives no artist's name; but if not directly after anything executed by Wright, was certainly imitated from him, and possesses enough of the characteristics of the Evans to entitle it and those resembling it to be classed therewith.

The print by Dawe presents an entirely different portrait, which it is extremely doubtful was ever painted by Wright. The figure is large and quite gross, the features coarse, and the whole appearance anything but pleasant. Its rarity is its only recommendation.

74. WRIGHT.

G. WASHINGTON. Bust in uniform, in profile to right. The Title, in a ribbon beneath the Bust. Oval. *Etched.*

Height 2 9-16 inches; width 1 15-16 inches.

J. Wright Pinx^t & F^t.

This is the original etching, executed by Joseph Wright, from a drawing, made in Trinity Chapel N. Y. in 1790. It was printed on a small card, and has become extremely rare, three impressions only, having come to the knowledge of the writer.

7

75. CHAPMAN.

GEORGE WASHINGTON President of the United States of America. Bust in uniform, in profile to right.   Oval, with narrow border.   *Stipple.*

Height 2 14-16 inches; width 2 3-16 inches.

Engraved from an original Drawing taken in New York in 1791. J. Chapman sculpsit.   *Extremely rare.*

A close copy of the Etching by Wright.   The date is an error.

76. COLLYER.

G. WASHINGTON.   Bust in uniform, in profile to right.   The Title, in ribbon beneath the Bust.   Oval.   *Stipple.*

Height 2 9-16 inches; width 1 14-16 inches.

Painted by J. Wright.   Engraved by J. Collyer.   *Extremely rare.*

A close copy of the Etching by Wright.

77. —— ——.

THE PRESIDENT OF THE UNITED STATES.   Bust in uniform, in profile to right.   Oval.   *Etched.*

Height 2 5-16 inches; width 1 13-16 inches.

"Massa. Mag."   (March No. 1791)   *Rare.*

A copy of the Etching by Wright.

78. —— ——.

GEORGE WASHINGTON, Died 14ᵀᴴ Dec. 1799 aged 68.   Bust in uniform, in profile to left.   Oval, with narrow border upon a Base, engraved to represent stone work.   At the top, partly within the border, a laurel wreath, which tied by a Ribbon extends down either side. The bottom and sides of the oval, surrounded by war Emblems.   Title upon the Base.   *Stipple.*

Height 4 8-16 inches; width 3 8-16 inches.

A close copy of the Etching by Wright. Only one impression has come under the notice of the writer.

79. —— ——.

Bust in uniform, in profile to right.   Oval.   *Lithograph.*

Height 2 14-16 inches; width 2 2-16 inches.

On the back of this print in eighteen irregular lines, is the following autograph fac-simile. "The Godlike WASHINGTON died 14th Decr 1799 *All America in tears.* The within is the best likeness I have seen. The hair is of his own head, this will increase its value with time. It is my earnest request this may be preserved to succeeding Generations. The hair was presented to me by Maj^r Billings Con. Army. E. Watson. *Certificate.* This may certify that the within hair was Enclosed by Genl Washington in a Letter to me dated Newburgh June '83, as his own hair. Jany 1. 1800 And^r Billings."

This drawing is a close copy of the Etching by Wright, and it is probable that the above inscription and Certificate, may have been written on the back of the impression, from which it was made.

80. DAWE.

GENERAL WASHINGTON LATE PRESIDENT OF THE AMERICAN CONGRESS. Three quarter length, in uniform, Head nearly in profile, the body three quarters to left. The right hand rests upon a sword hilt, held from the body and perpendicular therewith, a chapeau in the left. In the distance to the left, a Battle.

Height 19 inches; width 13 10-16 inches.

Painted by R. Wright of Philadelphia. P. Dawe sculpt. *London Published by D. Gally N° 263 High Holborn Jany 8th 1801.*

Extremely rare.

81. DOOLITTLE.

GEN. GEORGE WASHINGTON COMMANDER IN CHIEF OF THE ARMIES OF THE UNITED STATES, BORN FEB: 11TH 1732 O. S. DIED DECEMBER 1799. Bust in uniform, in profile to right. Over the head, an eagle with laurel wreath. Vignette.   *Stipple.*

Height 3 4-16 inches; width 1 5-16 inches.

A. Doolittle sculp. *Extremely rare.*

[The Majesty and Mortality of created Gods Illustrated and Improved. A Funeral Discourse Delivered at North-Haven December 29. 1799 on the Death of General George Washington who died December 14, 1799. By Benjamin Trumbull, D.D. New Haven 1800.]

A copy of the Etching by Wright.

82. —— ——.

G. WASHINGTON PRESIDENT OF THE UNITED STATES. Bust in uniform, in profile to left. Oval. *Etched.*

Height 4 4-16 inches; width 3 12-16 inches.

[Title Page to "The Battle of Prague Favorite Sonate for the Piano Forte." Boston Printed & sold by Graupner N° 6 Franklin St.]

From the Etching by Wright. Only one impression has come under the notice of the writer.

83. EVANS.

Full Bust in uniform, three quarters to right, Head in profile. Oval.

Stipple.

Height 4 6-16 inches; width 3 6-16 inches.

Drawn by J. Wright. Engraved by W. Evans.

[Heading to a Broadside Edition of The Farewell address. T. Bensley Printer, Bolt Court, Fleet Street London.] *Extremely rare.*

Subsequently printed in colors, the background having been removed. These impressions have the Title "General Washington" and the following address, "Published 1 March 1800 by Thos. Medland Abingdon Street Westmr."

84. —— ——.

Full Bust in uniform, three quarters to right, Head in profile. Oval, of a single line, no background. *Etched.*

Height 2 12-16 inches; width 2 1-16 inches.

Only one impression has come under the notice of the writer.

85. —— ——.

Full Bust in uniform, three quarters to right, Head in profile.   Ruled
background.   *Etched.*

Height 2 13-16 inches; width 2 4-16 inches.

[Force's Picture of the city of Washington.]

86. —— ——.

GENERAL WASHINGTON.   Full Bust in uniform, three quarters to
left, Head in profile.   Oval.   *Stipple.*

Height 3 3-16 inches; width 2 8-16 inches.

Parson's Genuine Edition of Hume's England.   *Engraved for J.
Parsons Paternoster Row May* 1795.

87. HOLLOWAY.

GENERAL WASHINGTON.   Full Bust in uniform, in profile to right.
Oval.   *Line.*

Height 3 10-16 inches; width 2 14-16 inches.

T. Holloway sculp.   "Literary Magazine."   *Published as the act
directs* 1 *Aug.* 1792 *by C. Forster, Poultry.*   *Rare.*

88. —— ——.

GENERAL WASHINGTON.   Full Bust in uniform, in profile to right.
Oval.   *Line.*

Height 3 9-16 inches; width 2 13-16 inches.

89. —— ——.

GENERAL WASHINGTON.   Full Bust in uniform, in profile to left.
Oval.   *Stipple.*

Height 3 9-16 inches; width 2 13 16 inches.

For the American Universal Magazine.   (Philadelphia Feby. 1797.)

90. LEHMAN.

G. WASHINGTON. Bust in uniform, in profile to right. Title, in a ribbon beneath the Bust. Oval. *Etched.*

Height 2 9-16 inches; width 1 14-16 inches.

J. Wright Pinx. G. A. Lehman sc. Amst.

A close copy of the Etching by Wright. Only one impression has come under the notice of the writer, and beneath it, is printed in ordinary type letters, fourteen lines of eulogistic verse in Dutch, signed P. H. Themmen M.D. The following translation, is kindly furnished by Joseph W. Drexel the owner of the print:—

> "Behold a speaking likeness of the allgreat hero,
> Of the noblest of men; therefore approach reverentially,
> Ye friends of mankind! and recognize in this father of his countrymen,
> A Cato in council; a Cæsar in the field;
> A second Solon, whene'er his country's interest is at stake;
> A Hercules, if the state is threatened by boisterous winds,
> Yet in peaceful times, but an humble farmer.
> At once the dread of Albion, and her object of esteem.
> A hero, knowing as well to fight desperately,
> As to avoid by his skill, a useless sacrifice of blood.
> A bulwark, before his land; an unclouded sun,
> In its heroic crown; a quarter of the earth,
> From the yoke of oppression, with skill and moderation he protected.
> The best friend of the people: the great Washington."

91. MURRAY.

GENERAL WASHINGTON. Full Bust in uniform, in profile to right. Oval. *Line.*

Height 2 1-16 inches; width 1 8-16 inches.

From an orig¹ Drawg. George Murray Sculpt. "Pocket Magazine." *Published by Harrison & Co. Octr. 1, 1795.*

92. O'NEILL.

GEORGE WASHINGTON. Bust, in profile to right. Vignette. *Mixed.*

Height 1 12-16 inches; width 1 3-16 inches.

Elias Dexter 564 Broadway (1863)

Engraved from a copy of the Etching by Wright, drawn by Joseph Ames of Boston, the military coat being changed into a civil one, the arrangement of the hair somewhat different, and the features considerably altered.

93. O'NEILL.

WASHINGTON. Full Bust, in uniform, Head to right.   *Mezzotinto.*

Height 5 inches; width 4 2-16 inches.

Engraved by J. A. O'Neill. From an original contemporary Picture in the possession of William Menzies Esq. *Private Plate.*

[Addresses of the City of New York to George Washington with His Replies. New York, 1867. Printed for Private Distribution.]

94. ROOSING.

WASHINGTON. Bust in uniform, in profile to right. Oval. *Stipple.*

Height 3 11-16 inches; width 2 14-16 inches.

H. Roosing sculp. Rotterdam. *H. Loosjes Pz. Excud¹ 1793.*

Very rare.

95. SCOLES.

GENERAL WASHINGTON. Full Bust in uniform, three quarters to right, Head in profile. Oval in a rectangle.   *Stipple.*

Height 2 12-16 inches; width 2 3-16 inches.

Scoles sc. *Published by Smith New York*   *Rare.*

96. SMITH.

G. WASHINGTON AS HE APPEARED WHILE REVIEWING THE CONTINENTAL ARMY ON BOSTON COMMON 1776. Bust in uniform, in profile to right. Oval medallion, in the centre of a rectangle ruled with waved lines, and inclosed by a border.   *Stipple.*

Height 5 14-16 inches; width 5 inches.

Drawn by N. Fullerton.   Engraved by G. G. Smith.   "Entered according to Act of Congress, in the year 1851, by Charles Fox in the Clerks Office of the District Court of Massachusetts."

[A Portrait of George Washington from an original Drawing.   A History of the Portrait, &c.   By Charles Fox.   Boston 1851.]

The writer of the pamphlet to which this print is prefixed, declares that it was executed, from "A Portrait of George Washington, as he appeared while reviewing the Continental Army on Boston Common in 1776," drawn by Nathaniel Fullerton, a young Artist of that city.   The pamphlet, was published, "To rescue from oblivion a Portrait which, in the opinion of competent judges, is a remarkable likeness of the Father of his Country," and contains Certificates as to its correctness in that respect, by a number of persons who had seen Washington in Boston, in the years 1776 and 1789.   As to the latter statement, we have but little doubt, feeling quite certain that the drawing from which the engraving was made, was a copy of the original etching by Joseph Wright, to which Fullerton had affixed his name, without any thought of claiming it for an original work, as the etching at the time of its publication (1790), seems to have been well known in the Eastern States.   A comparison of the etching and engraving, leaves no room to doubt, that this, is the true version of the matter, and that the Title of the print, is manifestly incorrect.

97. —— ——.

G. WASHINGTON.   Born Virginia Feb^{ry} 11th 1732 General of the American Armies 1775 Resigned 1783 President of the United States 1789.   Full Bust in uniform, in profile to left.   Title, in a ribbon on the arm.   Circle.   *Stipple.*

Diameter 3 9-16 inches.

A cotemporary print, and possibly a free copy of the head in the "Manly Medal," supposed to be by Wright.   It is rather a crude effort, and only one impression of the original state, has come under the notice of the writer.   The plate is still in existence, having been entirely worked over, the Title removed from the arm, and engraved in much larger letters in the upper margin.   The impressions from the altered plate, all taken comparatively recently, are well known to collectors.

ROBERT EDGE PINE.

Son of John Pine, engraver, was born in London in the year 1742. It is not known by whom he was instructed, but he gained the first premium offered by the Society for the encouragement of Arts, for the best historical picture painted in oil, figures life size, in 1760, and for the second time in the year 1762.

He afterwards practiced as a portrait painter both in London and Bath, and was considered a good colorist. Many of his theatrical portraits were engraved by McArdell, Valentine Green, Watson, and others, and were very popular.

Pine came to America in the year 1783, for the purpose of painting portraits of the heroes and patriots of the Revolution, in order to combine them in historical pictures commemorating the events of that period. He made his residence in Philadelphia, having brought letters of introduction to the Hon. Francis Hopkinson, whose portrait was the first he painted in this country. It was the letter of that gentleman to Washington, explaining Pine's design of collecting portraits for historical pictures, and requesting him to sit to the artist, which drew out the celebrated letter dated Mt. Vernon 16th May, 1785. "In for a penny, in for a pound, is an old adage. I am so hackneyed to the touches of the Painter's pencil, that I am now altogether at their beck, and sit like patience on a monument whilst they are delineating the lines of my face. It is a proof among many others of what habit and custom can effect. At first I was as impatient at the request, and as

8

restive under the operation, as a colt is of the saddle. The next time
I submitted very reluctantly, but with less flouncing. Now no dray
moves more readily to the Thill, than I do to the Painter's Chair. It
may easily be conceived therefore that I yielded a ready obedience to
your request, and to the views of Mr. Pine. Letters from England,
recommendatory of this Gentleman, came to my hand previous to his
arrival in America, not only as an Artist of acknowledged eminence,
but as one who had discovered a friendly disposition towards this
country, for which, it seems he had been marked."

Pine remained three weeks at Mt. Vernon, and besides that of
Washington, painted also the portraits of Mrs. Washington's Grandchildren. He executed quite a number of portraits in Philadelphia,
Baltimore, Annapolis, and in different parts of Virginia, all of which
are held in high esteem, but his project of painting the historical
pictures was never fully carried out.

Robert Edge Pine died at Philadelphia, November 19, 1788. His
family, a widow and daughters, returned to England.

We have but two engravings of this portrait, one by H. B. Hall en
vignette from the original picture, and the other by G. R. Hall taken
from an ornamental design by A. Chappel, the head being surrounded
by different objects referring to the civil and military history of Washington, as well as national allusions. The first named print, is the
most satisfactory as a transcript of the painting.

98. HALL.

WASHINGTON. Half length in uniform, Head three quarters to left.
The right hand rests upon a walking stick. Vignette.   *Stipple.*

Height 5 8-16 inches; width 4 inches.

II. B. Hall. From the original Picture from life by Robert Edge Pine taken in 1785. (In possession of J. Carson Brevoort Esq, Brooklyn N. Y.) *Engraved for Irving's Washington.*

[Life of George Washington. By Washington Irving. New York, 1856–59.]

99. HALL.

G. WASHINGTON. Bust in uniform, Head three quarters to left. Oval, in a frame adorned with laurel leaves, resting upon a Base in a rectangle. At the top of the Frame " E Pluribus Unum," and beneath it, an open scroll containing fac-simile autographs of the signers. *Stipple.*

Height 8 9-16 inches; width 6 4-16 inches.

Painted by A. Chappel. Engraved by G. R. Hall. From the original Portrait by Pine in the possession of J. Carson Brevoort Esqr. (Copy Right 1856.)

JEAN ANTOINE HOUDON.

1785.

WAS born at Versailles, March 20th, 1741. Having gained the first prize for Sculpture in the Royal Academy at Paris (1760), he visited Italy, where he passed ten years in the study of the Antique. After his return to Paris he was admitted to the Academy, and soon occupied a prominent position in his art.

In June, 1784, the General Assembly of Virginia passed a resolution, "That the Executive be requested to take measures for procuring a statue of General Washington, to be of the finest marble and best workmanship." In pursuance of this request, Governor Harrison commissioned Charles Willson Peale, to draw a full length picture of the General, directing him, when finished, to forward it to Paris, to the address of Thomas Jefferson, at that time a minister plenipotentiary with Adams and Franklin, to negotiate treaties of commerce with foreign nations.

The picture was painted and forwarded by the artist towards the end of the year, but Houdon, with whom Jefferson had contracted for its execution, was unwilling to undertake the statue without seeing Washington, and in consequence, arrangements were made for his doing so. He came to the United States in the same vessel with Dr. Franklin, arriving in Philadelphia in September of the following year.

Houdon reached Mt. Vernon the third day of October, and remained two weeks, during which time he made a cast of the face, from which

(60)

a bust was modelled, and took minute measurements of the person of Washington. He returned to Paris about the first of January, 1786, and the statue was completed in 1788, but the new Capitol at Richmond, in which provision was to be made for its reception, not being finished, it was detained in France to await that event. It was placed in position May 14th, 1796.

The Statue is of the exact size of life, six feet two inches in height, of fine Italian marble. The costume is the military dress of the Revolution. The right hand of the General rests upon a staff, the left is upon the folds of a military cloak thrown over the end of a bundle of fasces, with which are connected a sword and plough.

The inscription on the pedestal, which was written by James Madison, is as follows: "The General Assembly of the Commonwealth of Virginia have caused this Statue to be erected as a monument of affection and gratitude to George Washington, who, uniting to the endowments of the Hero, the virtues of the Patriot, and exerting both in establishing the liberties of his country, has rendered his name dear to his fellow-citizens, and given the world an immortal Example of true Glory."

The figure has been pronounced by Lafayette "a fac-simile of Washington's Person," while the bust, simple, yet dignified, grand, but full of humanity, is the acknowledged likeness, and stamped by Stuart, as the ideal of the great original.

Jean Antoine Houdon died at Paris, July 15, 1828.

Our List of prints includes but one of the Statue, and that executed from a daguerreotype, is neither very satisfactory as an engraving, nor faithful to the original. The bust, however, has been well en-

graved, and in the plates by Leney, and Durand, all the fine character, truth, and dignity of this master piece are preserved. The print by
Tardieu, which is now difficult to obtain, it having become very scarce
outside of early collections, is a beautiful example of engraving. But
perhaps the most interesting one, is that executed by an unknown
hand in the stipple manner, in imitation of a crayon sketch, No. 109.
It is peculiarly free and easy in the drawing, striking in expression,
and the whole character of the head and work, indicates the master
hand.

100. DURAND.

WASHINGTON. Profile Head and Bust, to right. Vignette. *Line.*

Height 3 4-16 inches; width 2 4-16 inches.

From Houdon's Bust. Engraved by A. B. Durand 1833.

[The Writings of George Washington. By Jared Sparks. Boston,
1834.]

101. HALL.

WASHINGTON. Profile Head and Bust, to right. Vignette. *Stipple.*

Height 3 4-16 inches; width 2 4-16 inches.

From Houdon's Bust.

[Life of George Washington. By Washington Irving. New York,
1856–59.]

102. HAMLIN.

WASHINGTON. Profile Head and Bust, to left, in a rectangle. Engraved by a Roulette.

Height 2 12-16 inches; width 2 1-16 inches.

Wm Hamlin sc. Æ. 91. From Howdan's Bust Richmond Va.

103. LENEY.

WASHINGTON.   Profile Head and Bust, to right, in a rectangle.
Stipple.

Height 5 inches; width 4 inches.

Drawn by J. Wood from Houdon's Bust.   Engraved by Leney.
Published by Joseph Delaplaine Chesnut S^t. Philad^n 1814.

[Delaplaine's Repository of the Lives and Portraits of Distinguished
American Characters.   Philadelphia, 1815–18.]

104. ORMSBY.

WASHINGTON.   Head in profile to left.   Oval medallion, suspended
by a ring, in a ruled rectangle.

Height 10 10-16 inches; width 9 2-16 inches.

Ormsby's Pentography.

105. PARKER.

GEO. WASHINGTON.   Full figure in uniform, standing upon a pedestal,
Head in profile to left.   The right hand rests upon the folds of a military cloak thrown over the ends of a Bundle of fasces, and the left upon
a walking stick.   Vignette.   *Stipple.*

Height 6 inches; width 2 8-16 inches.

From the Statue by Houdon, in the capitol, Richmond Va.   Daguerre-
otyped from the statue.   Geo. Parker.   *G. P. Putnam & Co.*

106. SAINT MEMIN.

WASHINGTON.   Head in profile to right, laureated.   Oval.

Height 10-16 inch; width 7-16 inch.

The impressions in the two sets of the works of Saint Memin, referred to in the
sketch of that artist, are the only ones known to the writer.

107. STORM.

G. WASHINGTON. Profile Head and Bust, to right.   Vignette.

Stipple.

Height 2 8-16 inches; width 1 8-16 inches.

From Houdon's Bust.   Engraved by G. T. Storm.

[Life of George Washington.   By Jared Sparks.   Abridged by the author.   Boston, 1840.]

108. TARDIEU.

G. WASHINGTON.   Head in profile to left, the hair flowing and tied by a ribbon.   Circular medallion, Title on the left.   *Line.*

Diameter 3 inches.

Dessiné et Gravé d'apres Houdon par Alexander Tardieu.

"Pour sauver son pays du pouvoir arbritaire
Washington combatti en guerrier valeureux
Mais il acquit bien plus qu'une gloire vulgaire
Il fut homme d'Etat humain et vertueux.

Par J. Castera"

* Deposé a la Bibliotheque Nationale le 9 Vendemaire an. 9.   *A Paris chez Alex. Tardieu Gr. de la Marine Rue de l'Université N° 296 au Depot National de Machine.*   *Rare.*

109. —— ——.

Profile Head and Bust, to right.   Vignette.   *Stipple.*

Height 6 inches; width 3 8-16 inches.

Very rare.

Engraved to imitate a crayon drawing.

110. —— ——.

Head in profile to right.   Circular medallion upon a Base, inscribed
"Born Feb. 22 A.D. 1732—Died Dec. 14, 1799;" a figure of Liberty
on the right, the U. S. shield on the left.   The centre of a circle ornamented with views at Mt. Vernon.   *Line.*

Diameter 2 1-16 inches.

Designed by H. Billings, Engraved by the American Bank Note Co.
(Copy Right by H. Barnes 1859.)

Published at Boston in 1859, surrounded by a frame made from wood, (oak,) grown
at Mt. Vernon.

9

JAMES PEALE.

1788-1795.

MINIATURE Painter, was a younger brother and pupil of Charles Willson Peale. He painted two original miniatures of Washington, the first, according to the date on the engraving of it by H. B. Hall, in the year 1788, and the other, in 1795. The former one, now in possession of the Washington Grays, (artillery corps,) of Philadelphia, resembles the head by Pine. Of the latter, we have no information, other than the statement by his nephew Rembrandt, that his uncle James, during the second and third sittings, accorded to him by Washington in the autumn of 1795, painted at his left hand, a miniature on ivory.

Mr. Peale also painted in oil. In the year 1786, his brother executed a portrait of Washington from life, for his Gallery. This portrait, James copied on a larger canvas, and added the figure in military costume, with an attendant and horse in the background. The picture, is in the possession of James Lenox Esqr. of New York, and is the one engraved by John Sartain, No. 112.

James Peale died at Philadelphia, in May, 1831, in the eighty second year of his age.

(66)

111. HALL.

G. WASHINGTON. Bust in uniform, Head nearly in profile to right.
Vignette. *Line.*

Height 3 4·16 inches; width 3 inches.

Eng⁴ by H. B. Hall N. Y. 1865. J. Peale Pinx, 1788. (*Private Plate.*)

112. SARTAIN.

Half length in uniform, Head three quarters to right, the right hand on
sword hilt. In the rear to left, a Tent partly visible, and in the right
back ground, an attendant with a horse. *Mezzotinto.*

Height 8 4·16 inches; width 6 4·16 inches.

Engraved by J. Sartain after the original Painting From Life by
James Peale.

[Washington's Farewell Address to the People of the United States
of America. Reprint from the original MS. in possession of James
Lenox. Privately Printed. New York, 1850.]

MADAME DE BREHAN.

1789.

SISTER of the Count de Moustier the French Minister to the United States, an accomplished writer and skilful amateur artist, accompanied her brother to this country, and passed a few days at Mt. Vernon in the autumn of 1788. She was a great admirer of Washington, and on the evening of the day of his inauguration as first President of the United States, (April 30, 1789,) the front of her brother's house in New York, was beautifully decorated with paintings by her own hand, suggestive of the past, the present, and the future in American History, which were illuminated by borderings of lamps upon the doors and windows.

Washington gave her a sitting, as appears by the following entry in his Diary: "Saturday, 3d. (October, 1789.) Walked in the afternoon, and sat about two o'clock for Madam de Brehan, to complete a miniature profile of me, which she had begun from memory, and which she had made exceedingly like the original."*

Madame de Brehan returned to France with her brother shortly afterwards, the President making an informal visit upon them for the purpose of taking leave, on the 14th of the same month. After their return, the Count had an engraving made from the original, proofs of

---

* The previous entry of this day is as follows: "Sat for Mr. Rammage near two hours to day, who was drawing a miniature picture of me for Mrs. Washington." This Portrait has not been engraved, and the whereabouts of the original is unknown.

(68)

which were sent by him to Washington, in May of the following year. One of these proof impressions, was presented by Washington to Mrs. Robert Morris, a grand-daughter of whom, in turn, presented it shortly after the battle of Antietam (1862), to General George B. McClellan. It was from this impression, that the engraving by Burt was executed.

Madame de Brehan also painted on copper in medallion form, the profiles of Washington and Lafayette accolated, and presented the picture to Mrs. Washington, after making a copy for herself. This is no doubt the medallion alluded to, in the Count's letter to Washington, of May 11, 1790, in which he refers also to sending the proof impressions of the prints. No engraving of this medallion has been executed; it has, however, been reproduced on wood, for " The Pictorial Field Book of the Revolution," and " The Home of Washington and its associations," by Benson J. Lossing.

Our list furnishes two engravings of the De Brehan miniature, those by Roger and Burt. The latter, a recent production, engraved as stated, from the proof impression presented by Washington to Mrs. Morris, varies somewhat from the former, the profile possessing more of the Houdon feeling, thus giving a head quite striking and characteristic. The print from which it was copied, we have been unable to see, nor do we know by whom it was executed.

The head by Roger, in reverse from the one by Burt, while not as manly in expression, and a little too much in the poetic order, is nevertheless an exceedingly interesting profile. Both of these prints are well engraved, and fill a valuable niche in a Washington collection.

113. ROGER.

GEORGE WASHINGTON NÉ EN VIRGINIE LE 11 FÉVRIER 1732. Profile Head to left, laureated. Circular medallion, in the upper part of a rectangle. The Title in a Tablet. *Stipple.*

Height 5 12-16 inches; width 4 inches.

Gravé d'apres le camèe peint par Madame de Bréhan à Newyork en 1789. Dirigé par P. F. Tardieu. Gravé par Roger.

[Voyage dans La Haute Pensylvanie et dans L'Etat de New York, Par un Membre adoptif de la Nation O'Neida. Traduit et publié par l'auteur des Lettres D'un cultivateur Americain. Paris 1801.] *Rare.*

114. BURT.

G. WASHINGTON. Profile Head to right, laureated. Vignette.

Line.

Height 2 8-16 inches; width 2 2-16 inches.

"The President's compliments accompany the enclosed to Mrs. Morris." Engraved and Printed at the Bureau Engraving & Printing. This profile of Washington is engraved from the original now in possession of Gen¹ Geo. B. McClellan, which was presented to Mrs. Morris by Gen¹ Washington, accompanied by a note, of which the above text is a true and exact fac simile.

CHRISTIAN GULAGER.

1789.

WAS born at Copenhagen, Denmark, in 1759. He seems to have turned his attention to art at an early age, receiving, when but seventeen years old, the prize medal of the Royal Academy of his native city, for painting and drawing, which carried with it the privilege of travelling for three years through Europe, at the King's expense, for the study of art.

Gulager came to America when about twenty-two years of age, settling in Boston, where he married and prosecuted portrait painting, opening a gallery for the exhibition of his own and other paintings, which is said to have occupied, an important place in the community.

When Washington visited Boston as President, on his eastern tour, in October, 1789, Gulager in the words of the Rev. Jeremy Belknap, "stole a likeness of him from a pew behind the pulpit," in King's Chapel, while listening to an oratorio performed in his honor. Not satisfied with this, it was made in pencil, the artist followed the Presidential party to Portsmouth, N. H., where, according to the following entry in Washington's Diary, he had a better opportunity, being accorded a regular sitting. "Tuesday, 3d. (Nov.) Sat two hours in the forenoon for a Mr. ——, Painter of Boston, at the request of M. Brick of that place; who wrote Maj. Jackson, that it was an earnest desire of many inhabitants of that town that he might be indulged."

Dr. Belknap, in referring to this incident, says: "He obtained a very good likeness; after which he laid aside the sketch which he took in the chapel; which, however, was not a bad one." This portrait, became the property of Daniel Sargent, Jr., who afterwards presented it to Dr. Belknap. At the time of its being engraved by Marshall, it was in the possession of a grandson, Edward Belknap; it is now owned by a great-grand-daughter, Mrs. Arthur Codman, of Bristol, R. I.

Christian Gulager left Boston in 1791, and after living in New York about nine years, went to Philadelphia, where he died in 1827.

The only engraving we have of this portrait, is the one by Marshall, which is well executed, and is said to be an excellent rendering of the original. The head, which is rather awkwardly drawn, possesses in general effect, some of the characteristics of the Savage, more noticeable in the print in that list, by an unknown engraver, inscribed as being from an original miniature in the possession of Benjamin Smith of Philadelphia.

115. MARSHALL.

GEORGE WASHINGTON.   Head and Bust, three quarters to right.
Oval in a rectangle.   *Line.*

Height 4 10-16 inches; width 3 13-16 inches.

Eng⁴ by Wm E. Marshall from a Portrait by Gulligher belonging to E. Belknap Esqr.

[Proceedings of the Massachusetts Historical Society, vol. i, 1855–58.]

EDWARD SAVAGE.

1790.

PAINTER and Engraver, in the Mezzotinto and Stipple manner, was born at Princeton, Mass., in the year 1761. His original calling was that of a goldsmith, which, however, he relinquished for portrait painting and engraving.

Having offered to execute a portrait of Washington as a gift to Harvard College, to be placed in the Philosophy Chamber, the President, at the request of that Institution, sat to him in the city of New York, three times, as appears by the following entries in his diary.

"Monday 21st. (Dec. 1789.) Sat from ten to one o'clock for a Mr. Savage, to draw my Portrait for the University of Cambridge, in the State of Massachusetts, at the request of the President and Governors of the said University."

"Monday 28th. Sat all the forenoon for Mr. Savage, who was taking my portrait."

"Wednesday 6th. (Jany. 1790.) Sat from half after 8 o'clock till 10 for the portrait painter, Mr. Savage, to finish the picture of me which he had begun for the University of Cambridge."

This Portrait, afterwards engraved by the artist himself in the Stipple manner, the first mentioned in the appended list, is still preserved in the collection of the college, and is described in the Catalogue as follows: " No. 4. GEO: WASHINGTON, b. 1732. d. 1799—L. L. D. 1776.

10 (73)

Artist, Edward Savage, 1790—Donor, Edward Savage, 1792—Presdt. United States, 1789–1797. First L. L. D. of Harvard College." The contemporary record of the Institution, dated August 30, 1791, also possesses some interest. "Voted. That the thanks of this Corporation be given to Mr. Edward Savage, for his polite and generous attention to this University, in painting a portrait of the President of the United States, taken by him from the life; and that Mr. Savage's brother, be requested to transmit to him this vote."

Savage went abroad the following year, and studied for a time in London, under Benjamin West, and afterwards visited Italy. He subsequently practiced at Philadelphia and New York. Edward Savage, died at his native place in July, 1817.

An examination of the prints bearing the name of E. Savage as painter and engraver, leads to the conclusion that the statements made by William Dunlap, in his sketch of the artist (Arts of Design Vol 1 pa 321), and which were evidently furnished by that erratic genius, John Wesley Jarvis, a pupil of Savage's, are manifestly incorrect. The assertion that David Edwin was the real engraver of these works, is proved to be an error, from the fact, that the first and third mentioned prints in the list, were published in London, respectively, in the years 1792 and 1793, and that Edwin was not known as an engraver, until his arrival in Philadelphia in December, 1797, being then about twenty-one years of age. Moreover, one is executed in Mezzotinto, a method which he never practiced, and the other, although in Stipple, is entirely different in manner from that of Edwin, whose style is well known.

What works Jarvis refers to, when he says "that he made all his masters pictures, engraved them, printed them, and delivered them to customers," is not apparent, for besides those enumerated below, no other prints bearing the name of Savage as painter and engraver, are known (at least to the writer), except one of General Knox, published in London, Dec. 1791, executed in the Stipple manner. The statement, that Edwin engraved "The Washington Family," published in 1798, and that Jarvis assisted him is also made, but the work resembles closely the head of 1792, and although in some respects, the drawing is open to criticism, yet it is a well executed print.

The portrait of Washington, as given in these prints, possesses an air of truthfulness and individuality, which warrants the assertion, that the artist was faithful to his original, and in sympathy with a character whose dignity he felt, so far as was in his power, must be preserved. The first described print, is from the picture painted in New York for the college, a military portrait, and the one executed in Mezzotinto, representing Washington as President, in full dress, examining a plan of the city of Washington, exists only as an engraving, no painting of it being known. Both are well engraved.

All the prints in the following list, with the exception of that by Bertonnier, and the one published by Rymer, engraver unknown, are copies of the plates engraved by Savage as above mentioned, those executed by Hamlin, from the Mezzotinto full three quarter length, varying in certain accessories, from the original. The head by Bertonnier, is probably from Savage, although in passing through the French crucible, it has become slightly transformed. The print published by Rymer, London, 1794, said to be taken from an original miniature in the possession of Benjamin Smith of Philadelphia, gives us a head, quite different in drawing and pose from the Savage, but the general characteristics are such, as to warrant the belief, that it must have been modelled to a great extent from his work.

The list presents but three prints executed by foreign engravers, all the rest being by Americans.

116. SAVAGE.

GEORGE WASHINGTON ESQ^R PRESIDENT OF THE UNITED STATES OF AMERICA. Full Bust in uniform, the order of the Cincinnati on the left breast. Head three quarters to the right. Oval, in a rectangle.
Stipple.

Height 5 4-16 inches; width 4 3-16 inches.

Painted & Engraved by E. Savage. From the original Picture Painted in 1790 for the Philosophical Chamber at the University of Cambridge, in Massachusetts. *Publish'd Feby 7, 1792 by E. Savage N° 29 Charles Street, Midd^x Hospital.* *Very rare.*

117. SAVAGE.

GENERAL GEORGE WASHINGTON. Full Bust in uniform, the order of the Cincinnati on the left breast. Head three quarters to the right. Oval, in a rectangle. *Stipple.*

Height 5 4-16 inches; width 4 3-16 inches.

Painted & Engraved by E. Savage.

[Washington's Monuments of Patriotism. Philadelphia, 1800.]

This is the preceding Plate, with a slight alteration in the arrangement of the hair, and more prominence given to the throat.

118. SAVAGE.

GEORGE WASHINGTON ESQ^R PRESIDENT OF THE UNITED STATES OF AMERICA. Nearly full length sitting, legs crossed, at a Table to the right, upon which is a Hat with large Rosette. Head three quarters to right.

A large chart upon the Table, is held by the right hand, the left arm rests upon it, the hand hanging over in front. The background is formed by a curtain, which drawn at the right, reveals the sky, and the lower portion of a pillar. *Mezzotinto.*

Height 18 inches; width 14 inches.

E. Savage pinx. et sculp. From the original Portrait Painted at the request of the Corporation of the University of Cambridge in Massachusetts. *Published June* 25. 1793 *by E. Savage N° 54 Newman Street.* *Very rare.*

119. SAVAGE.

GEORGE WASHINGTON PRESIDENT OF THE UNITED STATES OF AMERICA. Nearly full length sitting, legs crossed, at a Table to the right. (Same description as the preceding print.) *Mezzotinto.*

Height 18 inches; width 13 14-16 inches.

From the original Portrait Painted at the request of the Corporation of the University of Cambridge in Massachusetts.

This is a different Plate from the preceding one, although very similar. It is not so well executed, and slight differences are visible throughout, the most marked perhaps, being the Rosette on the Hat, which is entirely different. It is supposed to be by Savage. Only two impressions, have come to the knowledge of the writer.

120. SAVAGE.

THE WASHINGTON FAMILY. GEORGE WASHINGTON HIS LADY AND HER TWO GRANDCHILDREN BY THE NAME OF CUSTIS. LA FAMILLE DE WASHINGTON. GEORGE WASHINGTON SON EPOUSE ET SES DEUX PETITS ENFANTS DU NOM DE CUSTIS. Full figure in military costume, seated to the left of the print. His right arm, rests on the shoulder of the boy who is standing, while the left, is upon a chart extended on a Table, to a part of which, Mrs. Washington points with a fan. *Stipple.*

Height 18 6-16 inches; length 24 6-16 inches.

Painted & Engrav'd by E. Savage. *Publish'd March* 10th 1798 *by E. Savage & Robt Wilkinson N° 58 Cornhill London.* *Rare.*

121. BERTONNIER.

WASHINGTON. Bust in uniform, Head three quarters to the right.
Vignette. *Line.*

Height 3 inches; width 3 4-16 inches.

Marckl Del. Bertonnier sculp. *Publié par Pourrat F. A Paris.*

122. BUTTRE.

WASHINGTON. Full Bust in uniform, the order of the Cincinnati on
the left breast. Head three quarters to the right. Vignette.
Mezzotinto.

Height 4 8-16 inches; width 3 8-16 inches.

Eng^d by J. C. Buttre N. Y. after a painting by Edward Savage.

[Washingtoniana; or, Memorials of the Death of George Washington.
By Franklin B. Hough. Roxbury Mass. 1865.]

Copy of the Stipple Head by Savage No. 116.

123. HAMLIN.

GEN^L GEORGE WASHINGTON. Nearly full length in military coat,
sitting at a Table to the right, crossed legs. Upon a Pedestal to the
right relieved against the sky, an urn, with halo at top, bearing the Inscription "G. W. Obt. Decb^r 14th 1799 Æ. 68." On the side of the
Pedestal "The Grateful Tribute of his admiring countrymen," and on
the front in three lines, "Death ere thou hast slain another, Wise and
Great and Good as He, Time shall throw his dart at thee."
Mezzotinto.

Height 17 11-16 inches; width 13 14-16 inches.

E. Savage Pinx^t. Wm Hamlin sculpt. *Published July* 1800 *by W^m
Hamlin Providence R. I.*

A copy with the variations above noted of the Mezzotinto by Savage No. 118. One
hundred impressions only of this plate, were taken for subscribers. It has become extremely rare.

124. HAMLIN.

GEORGE WASHINGTON ESQ^R Ob^T Decb^R 14TH 1799. Æ. 68.
Nearly full length, sitting at a Table to the left, crossed legs, Head
three quarters to the left. *Mezzotinto.*

Height 7 5-16 inches; width 5 8-16 inches.

E. Savage pinxet. Wm Hamlin sculp. Providence.

Copy in reverse of the Mezzotinto by Savage No. 118. This plate is still printed from.

125. HAMLIN.

GEN^L GEORGE WASHINGTON Ob^T Decb^R 14TH 1799 Æ 68. Nearly
full length in uniform, sitting at a Table to the left, crossed legs. The
order of the Cincinnati on left breast. The waistcoat is unbuttoned,
and the hilt of a sword lies against the Table. An urn, surmounted by
a figure of Fame with Trumpet, is relieved against the sky.
Mezzotinto.

Height 7 4-16 inches; width 5 9-16 inches.

E. Savage pinxet. Wm Hamlin sculp. Providence.

Copy in reverse of the Mezzotinto by Savage No. 118, with the variations as above
noted. Only one impression, has come to the knowledge of the writer.

126. HAMLIN.

GEN^L GEORGE WASHINGTON. Bust in uniform, Head three quarters to right. Oval. *Stipple.*

Height 3 14-16 inches; width 3 3-16 inches.

E. Savage Pinx^t. Wm Hamlin sct. Prov^d. "Farnsworth's Edition."
Very rare.

[Memory of Washington. Newport, R. I. Printed by Oliver Farnsworth, 1800.]

127. HAMLIN.

GEN.ᴸ GEORGE WASHINGTON. Full Bust in uniform, Head three quarters to right. Oval, surrounded by rays.   *Stipple.*

Height 10-16 inch; width 7-16 inch.

128. HARRISON.

GEN.ᴸ GEO.ˣ WASHINGTON. Full Bust in uniform, Head three quarters to left. The order of the Cincinnati, on the right breast. Oval, in a rectangle.   *Stipple.*

Height 4 2-16 inches; width 3 inches.

W. Harrison Junᵣ sculpt.   *Very rare.*

[Legacies of Washington. Trenton, 1800.]

129. HILL.

GEORGE WASHINGTON, Pʀᴇsɪᴅᴇɴᴛ ᴏғ ᴛʜᴇ Uɴɪᴛᴇᴅ Sᴛᴀᴛᴇs ᴏғ Aᴍᴇʀɪᴄᴀ. Full Bust in uniform, Head three quarters to right. The order of the Cincinnati, on the left breast. Oval, in a rectangle.   *Stipple.*

Height 4 inches; width 3 inches.

Engraved by S. Hill.   *Rare.*

[Official Letters to the Honourable American Congress, written during the war between the United Colonies and Great Britain. 2nd Ed., Boston, 1796.]

130. HOUSTON.

GEORGE WASHINGTON ESQᴿ. Full Bust in uniform, the order of the Cincinnati, on the left breast. Oval.   *Stipple.*

Height 4 14-16 inches; width 4 2-16 inches.

Houston sc. *Philadᵃ Published for Thoˢ Condie Bookseller.* *Rare.*

[Philadelphia Monthly Magazine for 1798, Vol. 1.]

Copy of the Stipple Head by Savage No. 116.

131. O'NEILL.

WASHINGTON. Full Bust in uniform, Head three quarters to the left. Oval. *Stipple.*

Height 4 9-16 inches; width 3 8-16 inches.

Savage pinx. O'Neill sc. "Engraved for the Washingtoniana." *Published by Elias Dexter* 564 *Broadway N. Y.*

[Washingtoniana. Reprint N. Y. 1865.]

Copy of the Stipple Head by Savage, No. 116, omitting the order of the Cincinnati.

132. ROLLINSON.

GEORGE WASHINGTON PRESIDENT OF THE UNITED STATES. Bust in uniform, Head three quarters to left. The order of the Cincinnati, on right breast. Oval. *Stipple.*

Height 4 14-16 inches; width 3 12-16 inches.

Savage Pinxt. Rollinson sct. *Rare.*

[Epistles Domestic, Confidential, and Official, from General Washington. New York 1796.]

133. SARTAIN.

THE WASHINGTON FAMILY. (Copy of the print by Savage, No. 120.)
Mezzotinto.

Height 15 4-16 inches; length 22 14-16 inches.

Painted by Edward Savage. Engraved by J. Sartain.

134. SCOLES.

GEORGE WASHINGTON PRESIDENT OF THE UNITED STATES OF AMERICA. Nearly full length, sitting at a Table to the right, with crossed legs. *Line.*

Height 4 13-16 inches; width 3 12-16 inches.

I. Scoles del. et sculp. *Publish'd by Smith, Reed and Wayland.*

11

[An Historical, Geographical, Commercial and Philosophical, View of the United States of America and of the European Settlements in America and the West Indies. By W. Winterbotham. 1ˢᵗ Am. Ed. N. Y. 1796.]

Copy of the Mezzotinto by Savage, No. 118, the curtain in the background, being omitted.

135. TANNER.

G. WASHINGTON.   Full Bust in uniform, Head three quarters to the left.   Oval.   *Stipple.*

Height 4 12-16 inches; width 3 12-16 inches.

Savage pinx. Tanner sc.   "Engraved for the Washingtoniana."

[The Washingtoniana: Baltimore. Printed and sold by Samuel Sower. 1800.]

Copy of the Stipple Head by Savage, No. 116.

136. —— ——.

GEORGE WASHINGTON ESQ^R PRESIDENT OF THE UNITED STATES OF AMERICA.   Full Bust in uniform, Head three quarters to right.   The order of the Cincinnati, on the left breast.   Oval.   *Stipple.*

Height 5 inches; width 3 13-16 inches.

From the original Picture painted by Savage in 1790 for the Philosophical Chamber at the University of Cambridge in Massachusetts. *London Pub^d for the Proprietor Aug. 10th 1793 by E. Jeffery N° 11 Pall Mall.*   *Rare.*

Also printed in Tint.

137. —— ——.

GEORGE WASHINGTON PRESIDENT OF THE UNITED STATES OF AMERICA.   Bust in uniform, body slightly to left, head drawn in rather an awkward manner, three quarters to right.   Oval.   *Stipple.*

Height 4 inches; width 3 4-16 inches.

From an original miniature in the possession of Benjamin Smith of Philadelphia. *London Published by D. Rymer, Book & Print Seller* 10 *Broad Court, Long Acre.* *Extremely rare.*

The following address, also occurs, "Published June 10th 1794 by T. Palfer N° 4 Bridge Road Lambeth near the Turnpike." This portrait, is different in the pose of the head, and other essentials, from the Savage, but its general effect is such, as to entitle it to be placed in this connection.

JOHN TRUMBULL.

1790–93.

Son of Jonathan Trumbull, the revolutionary Governor of Connecticut, was born at Lebanon in that State, June 6, 1756. He received an excellent education, showing great facility in acquiring knowledge, particularly of languages, and graduated at Harvard College in July, 1773. At an early age a taste for drawing developed itself, and while at Cambridge, he copied a print after Coypel, which was shown to Copley, and commended by him.

Upon his return to Lebanon, he turned his attention to painting, but the mutterings of coming revolution exciting his enthusiasm, the palette was abandoned, and he became interested in military studies and exercises, entering the army as adjutant to the 1st Connecticut Regiment. He marched to Boston in May, 1775, and was stationed at Roxbury.

Understanding, that Washington was desirous of obtaining a correct plan, of the enemy's works on Boston Neck, the young adjutant commenced one, but the desertion of a British Artillery-man, who brought out with him a rude plan of the entire-works, prevented its being finished. Trumbull's drawing, however, was shown to the Commander-in-Chief, and attracted notice, in consequence of its correctness. He was soon after appointed aid-de-camp, and subsequently Major of Brigade.

In the following year, he accompanied the northern expedition under Gates, as adjutant, with the rank of Colonel, but becoming dissatisfied with the date of his commission, left the service in February, 1777, and returned to Lebanon; he afterwards went to Boston, to profit by studying the works of Copley and others, and while there, occupied the room which had been built by Smybert, in which remained many of his works.

In May, 1780, he sailed for Europe, being anxious to receive the benefit of instruction from Benjamin West, and after a short stay in Paris, reached London in the following August.

Mr. Trumbull has left us a list of drawings and pictures, (68 in number,) executed prior to his departure, which includes one, described as, "Gen. Washington, half length, from memory." He immediately went to work under West, who received him very kindly, but upon the receipt of the news of the death of Major Andre, he was arrested and committed to prison. His life was spared at the intercession of West, then high in favor with the King, but he remained confined for seven months, when he was liberated, on condition of quitting the kingdom within thirty days, West and Copley becoming his sureties. He proceeded to Amsterdam, and reached home in January 1782.

In the following November, Trumbull again embarked for England, where he pursued his studies indefatigably under Mr. West, remaining until the latter part of 1789, during which time, he painted his "Battle of Bunker Hill," and "Death of Montgomery," and arranged the compositions, for "The Declaration of Independence," "The Surrender of Cornwallis," and the Battles of Trenton and Princeton. He arrived at New York, Nov 26, 1789, and soon after, commenced painting portraits, to be introduced in these Historical pictures.

Washington sat to him seven times for this purpose, as appears by the following entries in his diary, and also rode with him upon one occasion, in order that the artist should see him mounted.

Wednesday, 10th. (Feby. 1790). Sat from 9 until 11 o'clock for Mr. Trumbull, to draw my picture in his historical pieces.

Friday, 12th. Sat from 9 o'clock until 11, for Mr. John Trumbull, for the purpose of drawing my picture.

Monday, 15th. Sat between 9 and 11, for Mr. John Trumbull.

Thursday, 18th. Sat for Mr. Trumbull from 9 o'clock till 10.

Saturday, 20th. Sat from 9 until 11, for Mr. Trumbull.

Saturday, 27th. Sat for Mr. Trumbull this forenoon.

March, 1790. Monday, 1st. Exercised on horseback this forenoon, attended by Mr. John Trumbull, who wanted to see me mounted.

Thursday, 4th. Sat from 9 until half after 10 o'clock for Mr. Trumbull.

In the summer of that year (1790), Trumbull painted for the city of New York, a full length portrait of Washington. This picture, which has not been engraved, is now in the Mayor's Office in the City Hall.

The artist, describes it in his autobiography as follows: "I represented him in full uniform, standing by a white horse, leaning his arm upon the saddle; in the background a view of Broadway in ruins, as it then was, the old fort at the termination; British ships and boats, leaving the shore, with the last of the officers and troops of the evacuating army, and Staten Island in the distance. Every part of the detail of the dress, horse, furniture, etc., as well as the scenery, was accurately copied from the real objects."

The full length painted by Trumbull, now in the " Yale School of

Fine Arts," at New Haven, and so well known through the engravings of it by Cheesman and Warner, was painted in Philadelphia. Its history, is also furnished us by the artist. " In 1792 I was again in Philadelphia, and there painted the portrait of General Washington, which is now placed in the gallery at New Haven, the best certainly of those which I painted, and the best, in my estimation, which exists, in his heroic military character. The city of Charleston, S. C., instructed William R. Smith, one of the representatives of South Carolina, to employ me to paint for them a portrait of the great man, and I undertook it *con amore* (as the commission was unlimited), meaning to give his military character, in the most sublime moment of its exertion—the evening previous to the battle of Princeton; when viewing the vast superiority of his approaching enemy, and the impossibility of again crossing the Delaware, or retreating down the river, he conceives the plan of returning by a night march, into the country from which he had just been driven, thus cutting off the enemy's communication, and destroying his depot of stores and provisions at Brunswick. I told the President my object; he entered into it warmly, and, as the work advanced, we talked of the scene, its dangers, its almost desperation. He *looked* the scene again, and I happily transferred to the canvas, the lofty expression of his animated countenance, the high resolve to conquer or to perish. The result was in my own opinion eminently successful, and the general was satisfied. But it did not meet the views of Mr. Smith. He admired, he was personally pleased, but he thought the city would be better satisfied with a more matter-of-fact likeness, such as they had recently seen him—calm, tranquil, peaceful.

"Oppressed as the President was with business, I was reluctant to ask him to sit again. I however waited upon him, stated Mr. Smith's objection, and he cheerfully submitted to a second penance, adding, 'Keep this picture for yourself, Mr. Trumbull, and finish it to your own taste.' I did so—another was painted for Charleston agreeable to their taste—a view of the city in the background, a horse, with scenery, and plants of the climate; and when the State Society of Cincinnati of Connecticut dissolved themselves, the first picture, at the expense of some of the members, was presented to Yale College."

Besides the portraits introduced in his historical pictures of "Trenton," "Princeton," "Surrender of Cornwallis," and "The Resignation at Annapolis," he painted in Philadelphia, in May, 1793, a head, the size of life; this is in the collection at New Haven. When the Hon. John Jay was appointed in 1794, envoy extraordinary to Great Britain, to negotiate a treaty of peace and commerce between the two nations, Trumbull accompanied him as secretary, and was afterwards appointed the fifth commissioner, to carry into execution the seventh article of the treaty. He returned to the United States in 1804, and resumed his pencil in New York. After another visit to London, of some duration, he finally returned to his native country in 1816.

The Trumbull collection, now in the building of "The Yale School of Fine Arts," Yale College, New Haven, contains Fifty-five pictures painted by him, conveyed to the College, December 19, 1831, in consideration of an annuity of one thousand dollars, to be paid during his natural life, and certain other stipulations as to their use and preservation.

Colonel Trumbull was President of the "American Academy of the

Fine Arts," for nine years, from 1816 to 1825. He died at New York, on the tenth day of November, 1843.

Trumbull makes no allusion in his autobiography, to the picture engraved by Valentine Green. According to the inscription of the print, it was published in 1781, the picture having been painted the previous year. The artist reached London on his first visit, in August, 1780, and lay there in prison, from November to June, of the following year. Upon his release he went to Amsterdam, and visited M. De Neufville (stated on the print to have been the owner of the painting), at whose house he resided until August, when he left for America, reaching home in June, 1782. The print must have been known to him, and the presumption is, that he painted the picture to please M. De Neufville, but was unwilling to acknowledge it. If executed by him, the measurements of the engraver being probably correct, it establishes one fact, that the former Aid placed a sufficiently high standard, upon his Commander-in-Chief. The head in this print, resembles Peale.

The figure, is repeated in the print by Misa, and in the one by an unknown engraver, bearing the additional title "Marshal of France," which appears on no other engraved portrait of Washington, and the head alone, in the print by Sherwin. The plate by Le Roy, is an exact copy of the Valentine Green. The print by Monin, is probably a variation of the full length, painted for the city of Charleston, some of the details, agreeing with the description of that picture, given by the painter himself.

With these exceptions, and the one by Blanchard, the engravings in the list, are all fair renderings of the Trumbull Portrait, at New

12

Haven. The whole picture, is best known through the excellent print by Cheesman, which is said to have been engraved under the superintendence of the artist himself, and the one by Warner, published in Philadelphia. The head by Durand, is a beautiful example of the burin, and the plate by H. B. Hall, engraved from a pencil sketch (Trumbull was peculiarly successful in this way), is one of that engraver's best efforts, and very satisfactory.

The print by Blanchard, in which a military cloak is thrown around the shoulders, is among the best engraved Washington portraits, but in expression, particularly noticeable about the mouth and eyes, is not very close to the original. It was engraved from a drawing by Couder, who seems to have taken some liberties with Trumbull.

138. BANNISTER.

G. WASHINGTON. Half length in uniform, Head to left.

Mezzotinto.

Height 4 10-16 inches; width 3 10-16 inches.

J. Bannister.

139. BLANCHARD.

WASHINGTON. Full Bust in uniform, a cloak around the left shoulder. Head to left. *Line.*

Height 8 6-16 inches; width 6 6-16 inches.

Dessiné par Couder. Gravé par A. Blanchard. "Dedic à S. E. le Général Jackson President des Etats-Unis d'Amerique, Par Son tres respectueux admirateur le Typographe N. Bettoni."

140. BURT.

WASHINGTON. Half length in uniform, Head to left. Vignette.

Etched.

Height 4 4-16 inches; width 3 4-16 inches.

[Washington and His Generals. By J. T. Headley. New York 1847.]

141. CHEESMAN.

GENERAL WASHINGTON. Full length in uniform, Head to the left, a field glass in the extended right hand, the left on sword hilt at his side. In the rear, a soldier with a horse, and in the extreme background, the representation of a battle, (Trenton.) At his feet, a dismounted cannon.

Stipple.

Height 25 6-16 inches; width 17 7-16 inches.

Painted by John Trumbull Esqr. Engraved by T. Cheesman. *London Published by A. C. De Poggi N° 91 New Bond Street June 1796.*

Rare.

Engraved under the superintendence of the Painter. Proofs, are before the outer dotted line of border. It was also printed in colors.

142. COUCHÉ.

G^{AL} WASHINGTON. Bust in uniform, Head to right. Vignette.

Etched.

Height 3 11-16 inches; width 3 4-16 inches.

Couché fils sc.

143. DAGGET.

WASHINGTON. Full length in uniform. (Fully described, in the Print by T. Cheesman, No. 141.) *Stipple.*

Height 5 2-16 inches; width 3 7-16 inches.

Engraved by A. Daggett from the original Painting by Colonel Trumbull. *Published by Nathan Whiting New Haven Con.*

[History of the War of Independence of the United States of America. By Charles Botta. New Haven 1834.]

Later impressions without the address, have the Title, "Washington at Trenton N. Jersey January 2^d 1777," and a reference to the painting, in five lines.

144. DURAND.

GEORGE WASHINGTON.   Half length in uniform, Head to left.
Line.

Height 4 8-16 inches; width 3 10-16 inches.

Eng. by A. B. Durand from the full length Portrait by Col. Trumbull belonging to Yale College.   (Copy Right 1834.)

[The National Portrait Gallery of Distinguished Americans.   Philadelphia 1834.]

145. GEOFFROY.

WASHINGTON.   Bust in uniform, Head to left.   Vignette.   *Stipple.*

Height 3 8-16 inches; width 3 8-16 inches.

Geoffroy sc. *Publié par Furne Paris.*

146. GIMBER.

GENERAL GEORGE WASHINGTON.   Bust in uniform, Head to left. Circular medallion, heading to an imperial folio sheet, containing "The Declaration of Independence," surrounded by Fifteen other medallions, two of which, contain Portraits of John Adams and Thomas Jefferson, and the others, the coats of arms of the thirteen original States.   *Stipple.*

Diameter 3 5-16 inches.

Published by Phelps & Ensign 7½ Bowery N. Y.

147. GREEN.

GENERAL WASHINGTON.   Full length in uniform, standing upon a rocky eminence near a river.   The right hand holding a hat, rests upon his sword hilt, while the left in which is a scroll, the arm across the body, is pointing to a fortification upon the opposite Bank.   In the bend of the river, in the rear, shipping enveloped in smoke, and to the right, a negro servant with a horse, browsing, his fore-parts only visible. In the lower margin, an Indian holding a shield, bearing the Washington Arms.   *Mezzotinto.*

Height 23 inches; width 16 inches.

Painted by J. Trumbull Esq' of Connecticut 1780.   Engraved by V.
Green Mezzotinto Engraver to his Majesty & to the Elector Palatine.
Engrav'd from the original Picture in the Possession of M. De Neuf-
ville of Amsterdam.   *Published by Appointment of M. De Neufville
Jany 15th 1781 by V. Green N° 29 Newman Street, Oxford Street Lon-
don.*   *Rare.*

148. HALL.

G. WASHINGTON.   Bust in uniform, Head to left.   Vignette, with a
background ruled to a rectangle.   *Etched.*

Height 4 12-16 inches; width 3 10-16 inches.

Etched by Alice Hall aged 18, New York 1866.

[Crumbs for Antiquarians.   By Charles I. Bushnell.   New York,
1864-66.   Privately Printed.]

149. HALL.

GEORGE WASHINGTON.   Bust in uniform, Head to left.   Vignette.
                                                Line.
Height 4 inches; width 4 4-16 inches.

Eng^d by H. B. Hall Morrisania N. Y. from the original by Col.
Trumbull.   (Private Plate.)

150. ILLMAN & SONS.

GEORGE WASHINGTON.   Full length in uniform, Head to left.
(Fully described, in the print by T. Cheesman, No. 141.)   Vignette.
                                                Line.
Height 10 inches; width 7 6-16 inches.

Engraved and printed by Illman & Sons.

151. LE ROY.

G. WASHINGTON.   Full length in uniform, standing upon an eminence
near a river.   Inclosed with a border, the Title in a Tablet in the lower
part.   *Line.*
Height 7 inches; width 4 9-16 inches.

J. Trumbull Pinx. Jᵃ le Roy sculp.

[Essais historiques et politique sur les Anglo-Americaines et sur la Revolution de l'Amerique Septentrionale Par M. Hilliard D'Aubertcuil. Bruxelles 1781.]

A copy in reverse, of the print by Valentine Green, No. 147. The border was removed, previous to its being used in the Book. It is extremely rare in the early state.

152. MISA.

GEORGE WASHINGTON Les Heros liberateur de sa patrie né en 1732 mort a la fin de 1799. Full figure in uniform, standing upon a rock near a river. The right arm is across the body, a chapeau in the left hand. To the left a Palm tree. *Line.*

Height 4 6-16 inches; width 3 inches.

Maria Misa sc.

A variation as respects the Landscape and omission of the horse, of the print by Valentine Green, No. 147. The objects are also quite diminutive.

153. MONIN.

WASHINGTON. Full length in uniform; in the extended right hand a field glass, the left on sword hilt at his side. In the left distance, a soldier with a horse, and a Palm tree in the right. Vignette. *Mixed.*

Height 6 inches; width 4 8-16 inches.

E. Monin sc. Guernied del.

Only one impression of this, has come under the notice of the writer.

154. READ.

G. WASHINGTON. Half length in uniform, Head to left. *Stipple.*

Height 4 inches; width 3 2-16 inches.

Eng. by Read from the full length Portrait by Col. Trumbull belonging to Yale College. *George Willis, Great Piazza, Covent Garden.*

[Life of George Washington. By John Corry. Dublin, 1801.]

155. ROGERS.

GENERAL WASHINGTON. Full length in uniform. (Fully described, in the print by T. Cheesman, No. 141.) *Line.*

Height 6 11-16 inches; width 4 9-16 inches.

Engraved by John Rogers from the Picture by Col. Trumbull.

[The Life of George Washington. By Benson J. Lossing. New York, 1860.]

156. SHERWIN.

GEN^L WASHINGTON. Bust, full face. Oval. *Line.*

Height 3 4-16 inches; width 2 12-16 inches.

Published according to the act of Parliament May the 10th 1783 by J. K. Sherwin N° 28 St James Street & Willm Hinton N° 5 Sweeting's Alley Cornhill. *Rare.*

Copy of the head, in the print by Valentine Green, No. 147.

157. TUCKER.

GEORGE WASHINGTON. Full length, in uniform. (Fully described, in the print by T. Cheesman, No. 141, but in reverse.) *Line.*

Height 6 14-16 inches; width 4 8-16 inches.

Engraved by W. E. Tucker from an original Painting.

[Pictorial Life of Geo. Washington. By J. Frost, L. L. D. Philadelphia, 1848.]

158. WARNER.

GEN. WASHINGTON (on the Battle Field at Trenton). Full length, in uniform. (Fully described, in the print by T. Cheesman, No. 141.) *Mezzotinto.*

Height 24 13-16 inches; width 17 8-16 inches.

Engraved by W. Warner from the original picture by Col. John Trumbull in possession of Yale College N. Haven. *Published by Wright & Graves Phila.* (Copy Right 1845.)

159. —— ——.

WASHINGTON.   Bust in uniform, Head to left.   Oval.   *Etched.*

Height 3 4-16 inches; width 2 10-16 inches.

160. —— ——.

HIS EXCELLENCY GEORGE WASHINGTON COMMANDER IN CHIEF OF THE AMERICAN ARMIES, MARSHAL OF FRANCE &C. Full length in uniform standing, an open scroll in his right hand, inscribed "Freedom established by Valour and Perseverance." The left arm is across the body. Beneath his feet, flags and two scrolls, marked "Stamp Act," and "Boston Port Bill," and near by, two Books labelled "Acts of Par." and "Brit. Stat." In the air, a figure of Fame with trumpet, advancing to the left, in the act of crowning him with a laurel wreath.

Line.

Height 6 8-16 inches; width 4 7-16 inches.

Extremely rare.

The figure in this, is the same as in the print by Valentine Green, No. 147, the accessories varied as above described.

ARCHIBALD ROBERTSON.

1791.

Was born near Aberdeen, Scotland, in 1765. He showed an early disposition for art, and after receiving a collegiate education, went to Edinburgh, in 1782, to study painting, associating himself with Raeburn, (afterwards so justly celebrated as a portrait painter), and some others, for the purpose of mutual improvement. After practicing his art in Aberdeen and Edinburgh, he went to London in 1788, and under the advice of Sir Joshua Reynolds, then President of the Royal Academy, gained admission to the schools. He afterwards returned to Scotland, and pursued his profession with success.

Being solicited to settle in America, he determined to come to the United States, and landed at New York on the second day of October, 1791.

In the month of December following, Robertson visited Philadelphia, then the seat of government, to deliver to President Washington, from the Earl of Buchan, the celebrated box made from the wood of the oak tree, which sheltered Sir William Wallace after his defeat at the battle of Falkirk, which had been intrusted to him for that purpose. In the letter presenting the box and introducing Mr. Robertson, the Earl requested that His Excellency would have the goodness to send him his portrait, that he might place it among those he most honored, and that he would like it to be from the pencil of Mr. Robertson.

13

The President, in compliance with this request, sat to Mr. Robertson for a miniature, on the afternoon of December 13, 1791, which was finished in January of the following year. From this, a large picture was painted in oil for the Earl, and transmitted to him, Washington referring to that fact in a letter to the Earl, dated May 1, 1792, in which he says, "The manner of the execution of it does no discredit I am told to the artist, of whose skill favorable mention has been made to me." The artist retained the miniature.

Mr. Robertson made New York his permanent residence, and followed his profession successfully for many years, confining himself to water colors and crayons, having found oil painting injurious to his health. He died at an advanced age.

Of the five prints included in the following list, only one, that by Dudensing, is inscribed as being after the Robertson miniature, the others, all by foreign engravers, while not presenting precisely the same portrait, bear some resemblance to it, and to each other, and are therefore classed therewith.

161. BOLT.

G. WASHINGTON 1796. Bust, head three quarters to right. Oval.
Stipple.

Height 2 14-16 inches; width 2 3-16 inches.

F. Bolt f. 1796. *Rare.*

162. DUDENSING.

GEORGE WASHINGTON. Bust, head three quarters to right. Oval. *Stipple.*

Height 3 8-16 inches; width 2 14-16 inches.

From the original miniature on Ivory, Painted from life by Arch[d] Robertson, in Philadelphia, in December 1791. *Elias Dexter*, 564 *Broadway New York*, 1866.

163. GRAINGER.

GEO. WASHINGTON. Bust, head three quarters to right. Oval, with border upon a Pedestal, in a rectangle, a large open scroll in front. To the right a sword and scales, and to the left a Liberty cap, and oak branches.   *Line.*

Height 7 inches; width 4 inches.

Grainger sculpt. *Published as the act directs July* 1. 1794 *by H. D. Symonds Paternoster Row.*

[View of the American United States. By W. Winterbotham. London, 1795.]

164. GRAINGER.

GEO. WASHINGTON. Bust, head three quarters to right. Oval.
                                                 Line.

Height 3 10-16 inches; width 2 13-16 inches.

W. Grainger Sculp[t]. *Published as the act directs Oct.* 25. 1794 *by H. D. Symonds Paternoster Row.*

[View of the American United States. By W. Winterbotham. London, 1795.]

165. KRETHLOW.

GEORGE WASHINGTON. Bust, head three quarters to right.
                                                Stipple.

Height 3 5-16 inches; width 2 9-16 inches.

Nach Frey. gest. V. Krethlow. *Zwickau, b. d. Geb. Schumann.* 1818.

GIUSEPPE CERACCHI.

1792.

Was born in Corsica about the year 1740, and when quite a youth, went to Rome to become a sculptor, studying under Canova. He attained a high rank in the art, and was employed by the Pope in conjunction with his master, in designing and executing works for the Pantheon.

In 1772, Ceracchi visited London and was well received, executing among others, a bust of Sir Joshua Reynolds then President of the Royal Academy.

An ardent Republican, Ceracchi conceived the design of executing a monument to Liberty in America, and for this purpose crossed the Atlantic. He arrived at Philadelphia in the year 1791, and prepared the model of a great work, designed to be one hundred feet in height, of statuary marble, and the cost was estimated at thirty thousand dollars. Washington favored the design, but Congress however did not feel itself authorized to expend money in such a manner, and the sculptor was disappointed.

Ceracchi modelled a bust of Washington from life. This head, although rather severe in style, is claimed to be an admirable representation of the hero, and the man. The mouth, is particularly remarked for its fidelity of expression.

It was purchased by the Spanish Ambassador as a gift to the Prince

(100)

of Peace, then at the height of his power at Madrid; before the bust reached Spain, Godoy was exiled, and the minister recalled, who on his arrival transferred it to Richard Meade Esqr. of Philadelphia, in whose family it remained until 1857, when it was purchased by Gouverneur Kemble of New York. He also repeated it in colossal size, a cast of which, was for a long time, in the New York Academy of Fine Arts.

Ceracchi returned to Europe in 1795. He entered into a conspiracy against Napoleon, was detected, and guillotined on the thirtieth day of January 1802.

We have but two prints after this Bust, those by Prud'homme and H. B. Hall, the latter being the most characteristic, and the best known.

166. HALL.

WASHINGTON.   Bust in profile to left, Head filletted.   Vignette.
Stipple.

Height 3 6-16 inches; width 3 inches.

H. B. Hall.   From the Bust by G. Ceracchi taken from life (now in possession of Gouverneur Kemble Esqr. Cold Spring.)   *Engraved for Irving's Washington.*

167. PRUD'HOMME.

WASHINGTON.   Bust, upon a pedestal, Head nearly in profile to left. Vignette, inclosed by a single line.   *Stipple.*

Height 3 9-16 inches; width 2 14-16 inches.

Drawn by J. G. Chapman from the original bust by Cerraci.   Engv'd by J. F. E. Prud'homme.

[A Life of Washington.   By James K. Paulding.   New York, 1835.]

———— WILLIAMS.

ON the second day of July 1792, Mr. Williams, (his Christian name is not given), presented to the First President, a letter of introduction from Henry Lee Governor of Virginia, favoring a desire on the part of the bearer, to paint the portrait of His Excellency. This, Washington refused, as appears by the following letter to the Governor dated at Philadelphia the following day, (July 3rd).

"Dear Sir. Your letter of the 20th ultimo was presented to me yesterday by Mr. Williams, who as a professional man may or may not be for aught I know, a luminary of the first magnitude. But to be frank, and I hope you will not be displeased with me for being so, I am so heartily tired of the attendance, which, from one cause or another has been given to these people, that it is now more than two years since I have resolved to sit no more for any of them, and have adhered to it, except in instances where it has been requested by public bodies or for a particular purpose (not of the painters), and could not without offence be refused. I have been led to make this resolution for another reason, besides the irksomeness of sitting, and the time I lose by it, which is, that these productions have in my estimation been made use of as a sort of tax on individuals, by being engraved, and that badly, and hawked about or advertised for sale."

Mr. Williams however persevered in his purpose, and acting upon the hint conveyed in the above quoted letter, offered to compliment the Alexandria Washington Lodge, (Masonic), No. 22, with a Portrait of the President, provided they would make application to him, for that purpose. This offer was brought before the Lodge at a meeting held August 29, 1793, and being received with favor, the application was ordered to be made.

Being thus armed, Mr. Williams met with better success than in his first effort, as appears by the following extract from the records of the Lodge, October 25, 1794. "Mr. Williams having offered to the Lodge a drawing of our worthy Brother George Washington President of the United States, the same is received, and in consequence of the trouble and expense Mr. Williams was at in going to and coming from Philadelphia, it is proposed that the members of the Lodge pay him Fifty Dollars, to be raised by voluntary subscription."

The artist, not satisfied with this amount, asked in the following month for further compensation, which however was refused, the Lodge considering the Fifty Dollars in the light of a gratuity, inasmuch as the application to the President was made at the request of Mr. Williams, who proposed should it be successful, to compliment them with the portrait, promising himself great pecuniary advantage by the sale of copies.

This portrait, which is inscribed on the back of the canvas, "His Excellency George Washington Esquire President of the United States, aged 64—Williams Pinxit ad vivum in Philadelphia, September 18, 1794," is in possession of the Alexandria Washington Lodge, No. 22, and was engraved for a frontispiece to a work by Sidney Hayden, entitled, "Washington and his Masonic Compeers," from which we make the quotations.

This Masonic portrait, which represents Washington with the collar and jewel of a Past Master, if fairly rendered in the print by O'Neill, is such a feeble attempt almost amounting to a caricature, that we are not surprised at the refusal of the Lodge to pay the painter of it, any thing more than his travelling expenses. However valuable it may be in the estimation of the order, the knowledge of such a production should have remained among the *arcana* of the Lodge Room, and it is to be regretted, that it was thought proper to engrave it.

168. O'NEILL.

WASHINGTON. Half length, in Masonic dress as a Past Master, head to right. Vignette. *Mixed.*

Height 5 inches; width 4 inches.

O'Neill N. Y. Engraved from the Portrait, painted from life by Williams, for Alexandria Washington Lodge, N° 22, Virginia, 1794.

[Washington and his Masonic Compeers. By Sidney Hayden. New York, 1866.]

WALTER ROBERTSON.

1794.

Who, according to Dunlap, was an Irish gentleman, came to America in the same vessel with Gilbert Stuart upon his return in 1793, landing at New York.

Robertson went to Philadelphia in advance of Stuart, and painted a miniature of Washington, which Robert Field, a miniature painter as well as an engraver, refers to in a letter to Robert Gilmore of Baltimore, dated Philadelphia, January 13, 1795, as follows: "Mr. Robertson's miniature of the President is as good a likeness and as fine a piece of painting as I ever saw. I have engaged to engrave it the same size with some ornaments to surround and make it more interesting, but as Mr. R. is determined to go to India early in the summer, he has declined the large plate, and offers to sell me the picture, which I should be glad to purchase, if the price he asks was not so extravagant, (viz. 1000 Dolls.) tho' it might be worth while even on those terms, if it was in my power. I have assistance offered me, but am fearful to engage so largely."

Dunlap, in speaking of Robertson, doubts whether Washington sat for this portrait, one reason being given that he is represented with a black stock, an article of dress which he affirms, Washington never wore, but besides the positive assertion that it was a good likeness and well painted, the tone of Field's letter indicates that *he* considered it an original.

14   (105)

This miniature, only known to us through the engraving by Field, represents Washington in uniform with a black neckerchief, the coat drawn together by a single button. The head is well drawn, the face full and rounded, and in some respects it resembles the last portrait by the elder Peale, painted in the autumn of 1795. The engraving is well executed, the ornamentation for the plate being designed by J. J. Barralet, an eccentric fellow countryman of Robertson's residing in Philadelphia.

Robertson subsequently went to the East Indies, where he died.

Robert Field the engraver of this print, an Englishman by birth, was an excellent miniature painter. He painted two copies of Stuart's first portrait of Washington, which are admirable examples of the art. One of these, was presented by Mrs. Washington, after the decease of her husband, to Tobias Lear his private Secretary; it is now in possession of his grand-daughter, Mrs. Wilson Eyre, of Newport, and the other, which was painted for Thomas Meredith, son of Samuel Meredith, first Treasurer of the United States, is now owned by Charles C. Moreau, of New York. Field practiced in Boston, Philadelphia, and Baltimore, and was at Mt. Vernon in 1798. He went to Canada about the commencement of the century, studied theology, was ordained a priest of the established church, and finally became a Bishop.

The prints by Houston and Tisdale in the following list, vary considerably from the one by Field, but although much changed, they appear to be founded on it; that by Tisdale omits the black neckerchief. The others are copies of the Field.

169. FIELD.

GEORGE WASHINGTON PRESIDENT OF THE UNITED STATES. Full Bust in uniform, with black neckerchief, Head to right. Oval, with narrow scroll border. On the point of a straight sword, which extends from the top of the oval, is a liberty cap, and across the middle the word "Libertas," surrounded by a laurel wreath; rays diverge from the wreath, losing themselves in clouds. Beneath the oval an eagle in clouds, with a long ribbon in his mouth the ends over his wings, inscribed "E Pluribus Unum." At each side, flags and palm branches reaching to the top. The whole, inclosed with two slight lines.

Stipple.

Height 11 13-16 inches; width 9 3-16 inches.

Painted by W. Robertson. Jon. Jas. Barralet Invenit 1795. Engrav'd by R. Field. *Published by Walter Robertson, Philadelphia & New York 1st August 1795.*

Only two impressions of this print, have come under the notice of the writer.

170. —— ——.

GEORGE WASHINGTON PRESIDENT OF THE UNITED STATES. Full Bust in uniform, with black neckerchief, Head to right. Oval, with narrow scroll border. Above the oval, a star with rays, and beneath, an eagle in clouds, with a long ribbon in his mouth the ends over his wings, inscribed "E Pluribus Unum." At each side, flags and palm branches reaching to the top. The whole, inclosed with two slight lines.

Stipple.

Height 11 4-16 inches; width 9 inches.

Robertson Pinxt. Walker Excudit.

Very rare.

With the exception of the star, in place of the sword above the oval, this is a close copy of the preceding print.

171. HOUSTON.

GENERAL WASHINGTON, PRESIDENT OF THE UNITED STATES OF AMERICA. Bust in uniform, with black neckerchief, Head slightly to right. In the lower margin, a figure of Liberty seated upon an Eagle, bearing a shield (the Washington Arms), and at her feet a cornucopia. To the right, a liberty cap upon an upright sword. Oval, in a rectangle.   *Stipple.*

Height 10 inches; width 8 2-16 inches.

J. J. Barralet del. H. Houston sculpt.

Only one impression of this, has come under the notice of the writer. It is in the "Phillips Collection" of engravings, "Pennsylvania Academy of the Fine Arts."

172. ROLLINSON.

G. WASHINGTON, PRESIDENT OF THE UNITED STATES.   Full Bust in uniform, with black neckerchief, Head to right. Oval.   *Stipple.*

Height 3 13-16 inches; width 2 14-16 inches.

Rollinson sculpt.   *Publish'd by I. Reid New York* 1796.

[An Historical, Geographical, and Philosophical View of the United States of America, &c. By W. Winterbotham. 1ˢᵗ Am. Ed. New York, 1796.]

173. TISDALE.

GENˡ WASHINGTON.   Full Bust in uniform, Head and Bust three quarters to left.   Oval, with border in a rectangle; beneath the oval, a representation of a review, entitled "Genˡ Washington takes command of the American Army at Cambridge July 3ᵈ 1775."   *Line.*

Height 6 8-16 inches; width 3 14-16 inches.

Tisdale sc. Engrav'd for C. Smith N. York.   *Very rare.*

[The American War from 1775 to 1783, with Plans. By Charles Smith. New York, 1797.]

174. —— ——.

GENERAL GEORGE WASHINGTON.   Full Bust in uniform, with black neckerchief, Head to right. Oval, with narrow scroll border.
                                                                Stipple.

Height 4 4-16 inches; width 3 7-16 inches.

                                                                Very rare.

[Dublin University Magazine.]

SAMUEL FOLWELL.

1795.

MINIATURE Painter, of whom little is known, was practicing his art in Philadelphia, the latter part of the last, and the beginning of the present century. The Profile of Washington in the possession of the " Historical Society of Pennsylvania," inscribed *S. Folwell Pinxt.* 1795, is said to have been taken upon a public occasion, the President being unaware of the fact. It is drawn on paper, and solidly painted in India ink, with certain lights touched in, and as declared at the time, is certainly a most spirited and correct likeness.

There is no engraving of this profile, but it has been reproduced on wood the same size as the original, height 3 12-16 inches, width 2 2-16 inches, Vignette, and published in "Annals and occurrences of New York City and State in the olden time," by John F. Watson. (Philadelphia 1846.)

ADOLPH ULRIC WERTMULLER.

PORTRAIT and figure painter, a native of Sweden, was born at Stockholm, about the year 1750, and after acquiring the rudiments of art at home, went to Paris, where he studied and pursued his profession for several years.

He gained considerable reputation, was elected a member of the Royal Academies of sculpture and painting, at Paris and Stockholm, and accumulated a respectable fortune, a greater part of which, was however lost in the financial troubles, of the early part of the French revolution.

Wertmuller came to America in May, 1794, landing at Philadelphia, where he was well received. Some time during the following year, although a member of the family has questioned and indeed almost positively denied the statement, Washington is said to have given him a single sitting. This portrait, of which the artist made several copies, afterwards came into the possession of Mr. Cazenove, a Swiss gentleman, who carried it with him upon his return to his native country. At the time of its being engraved by Hall it was owned by Charles Augustus Davis of New York, since deceased, who had purchased it a short time previous, from the grand-daughter of Mr. Cazenove.

Wertmuller remained in this country until the autumn of 1796, when he returned to his native place, remaining there several years. Being again unfortunate in pecuniary matters, he re-embarked for America, arriving at Philadelphia, in 1800, and in the following year, married a grand-daughter of Hesselius, Pastor of the Swedish congregation at Wilmington, Delaware, who brought him some property. Shortly after his marriage, Wertmuller purchased a farm below Marcus Hook on the Delaware, where he died October 5, 1811.

From this portrait, which, though well executed, cannot be considered a characteristic likeness, lacking force and elevation, we have two engravings. In the one by Buttre, a military coat has been added; this is incorrect, as the painting by Wertmuller represents Washington as a civilian. The print by Hall, which is the best, furnishes a good idea of the original.

175. BUTTRE.

GEORGE WASHINGTON.   Bust in uniform, Head to right.   Vignette.
Stipple.

Height 4 8-16 inches; width 4 inches.

Engraved by J. C. Buttre.   From the Portrait by Wertmuller.

176. HALL.

G. WASHINGTON.   Bust, head to right.   Vignette.   *Stipple.*

Height 5 8-16 inches; width 5 inches.

A. Wertmuller S. Pt. Phila. 1795.   H. B. Hall.   From the original Picture in the possession of Chas. Aug. Davis Esq. N. York.   *New York G. P. Putnam & Co.*

[Life of George Washington.   By Washington Irving.   New York, 1856–59.]

GILBERT STUART.

1795-96.

THIS eminent Portrait painter was born at Narragansett, Rhode Island, December 3, 1755. His first lessons in art, were received from a Scottish painter named Cosmo Alexander, and by whom, when about eighteen years of age, he was taken to Edinburgh. His stay was, however brief, and upon his return, he practiced his art at Newport and Boston, but the war interfering with his prospects, he decided to transfer his easel to London, as a better field for operation.

Here he received both aid and instruction from Benjamin West, who may not inaptly be termed, the *Mecca* of American painters, for all who were able to study abroad, seemed to turn to him, as their sure salvation.

Stuart soon became known, and his portraits were highly esteemed. After painting in London for some years, he went to Dublin about the year 1788, where he painted many of the nobility. He returned to America in 1793, the love for his own country, his admiration of General Washington, and the very great desire he had to paint his portrait, being the inducements to turn his back upon his good fortune in Europe. Landing in New York, he was kept constantly employed, until in furtherance of his purpose, he went to Philadelphia.

In the autumn (September,) of 1795, Stuart painted from life, his first portrait of Washington, and during the sitting, as he himself says, could find no subject, although he tried many, of sufficient interest to elicit the expression, he knew must accord with such features, and such a man.

This portrait, in which the head is to the right, not proving satis-factory to the painter, was afterwards, as declared by himself, destroyed or rubbed out. Rembrandt Peale, however, has stated on the au-thority of Dr. Thornton, of the Patent Office, who was intimate with Stuart, that after five copies of it were made, it was sold to Winstanley, an English landscape painter, then in this country. Winstanley took it to London, where it was bought by Mr. Samuel Vaughan, after whose death it passed into the possession of the late Joseph Harrison, Jr., of Philadelphia. In connection with this statement, may be taken the inscription on the first engraved plate after Stuart, published in Lon-don, Nov. 2, 1796, which is as follows: "Engraved by S. Holloway, from a Picture painted by Mr. Stuart in 1795, in the possession of Sam-uel Vaughan Esqr." An impression from this plate, having been com-pared with the picture still in the possession of the Harrison family, substantiates the fact of its being an exact rendering of that Portrait.

One of these copies, afterwards touched upon from life, became the property of Colonel George Gibbs, a warm and intimate friend of the painter; it is now owned by his nephew, Dr. William F. Channing, of Providence, R. I.* This is the portrait engraved from by Burt, which, while presenting an exceedingly fine production of the burin, has, through its faithfulness as a translation, made us familiar with an ef-

---

* We are indebted to George C. Mason Esqr. of Newport R. I. author of the forthcoming "Life and Works of Gilbert Stuart," for the information respecting this Portrait, and also, for the dates of birth and death of the artist.

15

fort of Stuart's, scarcely less important than the well known "Athen-æum Head," and certainly possessing marked traits of individuality.

On the twelfth of April, 1796, Washington, at the request of Mrs. Bingham, sat to Stuart for a full length, to be presented to the Marquis of Lansdowne. For this picture, Stuart is said to have had but one sitting, the figure being painted from a person shorter in stature than Washington. Simultaneously with this, he executed one for Mr. Bingham, owned by "The Pennsylvania Academy of the Fine Arts," and another for William Constable, now in the possession of his Grandson, Henry E. Pierrepont Esqr., of Brooklyn, N. Y.

Stuart subsequently painted another full length, but not from life, in which the right hand is resting upon the table and not extended, as if speaking, as in the Lansdowne picture. This is known as the "Tea Pot Portrait," from the disposition of the arms, and of which he made several replicas. Two of these pictures, are in the State Houses at Providence and Newport, R. I., one at Hartford, Conn., and another is owned by Robert Lenox Esqr., of New York. In these, the figure is turned more to the left, and is much better drawn than in the Lansdowne. Another full length, also not from life, is in military costume, standing by a horse; it is in Faneuil Hall, Boston, and represents Washington at Dorchester Heights.

After the picture was completed for Lord Lansdowne, Washington gave him a commission to paint the portraits of Mrs. Washington and himself. This portrait, known as the "Athenæum Head," was purposely left unfinished, and retained by the artist with the consent of Washington, the distinguished sitter being satisfied with a copy of it.

The original, which was never afterwards touched upon, but left vignette, in the same state as when the eyes of Washington rested upon it, was purchased after the death of Stuart, from his widow, in October, 1831, by the Washington Association of Boston, and other subscribers for fifteen hundred dollars, and presented to the Boston Athenæum.

Stuart made many copies of this head, always adding the bust, and it has been engraved time and time again. It is the best known of all the Washington portraits, and will doubtless retain its hold in the popular mind, as the standard head. Stuart himself, however, considered it inferior to the Houdon bust, placing that first, and *his* head next. In making this statement, he at the same time referred to the fact that when he painted it, Washington had just had inserted a set of false teeth, which accounted for the constrained expression so noticeable about the mouth and lower part of the face, and that the Houdon bust does not suffer from this defect.

Washington Allston, in an obituary notice of Stuart, published a few days after his decease, speaks of this head as follows: "A nobler personification of wisdom and goodness, reposing in the majesty of a serene conscience, is not to be found on canvas." We doubt, whether any other form of expression, could convey a more complete realization of this remarkable production.

After Congress removed to Washington, Stuart painted in that city for a few years, and then, in 1806, went to Boston, which place he made his permanent residence. Gilbert Stuart (he dropped a middle name, Charles, in early life) died July 27, 1828.

The engravings after Stuart comprise very nearly one-half the numbers of our Catalogue, and candor compels the statement that but few of them present good renderings of the originals. Quite a number of those executed for books, possess but little artistic merit, and seem to have been engraved either from bad copies, or from other prints, in themselves not much better. Of the book plates engraved and published in this country in the early part of the century, much however, should not be expected, as our engravers of that time can scarcely be classed as real practitioners, their opportunities for acquiring any positive knowledge of the art being exceedingly slight, and the remuneration in a corresponding ratio.

The first engraving of the "Lansdowne Portrait," executed by Heath, and from which, perhaps, most if not all the others of the whole picture were copied, although not one of his best plates, is a good rendering of the original. The reputation of the engraver, its early publication and extensive circulation, have made it familiar to all, and its position in public estimation is assured and lasting. The publication of this print without the knowledge of Stuart, was a great disappointment and a source of considerable annoyance to him, inasmuch as he had arranged with Mr. Bingham for the reservation of the copyright. Of this, the Marquis of Lansdowne was not informed, an omission on the part of Mr. Bingham which the artist never forgave. The head and bust from this portrait, has been well given in the prints by Holl, Fittler, Fenner, Sears & Co., Ormsby, and Edwards.

The best and most pronounced engravings after the "Athenæum Head," are those by Durand, Andrews, Marshall, Welch, and H. Wright Smith, the first three named being among the finest examples of engraved portraiture as yet executed in this country, and all, close translations of the original.

The first portrait painted by Stuart, known as the "Vaughan Portrait," is well rendered in the prints by Holloway and Ensom, those by Ridley and Mackenzie, which appear to be from the same picture, being widely different. Of the full-length, known as the "Tea Pot Portrait," several engravings will be found in the appended list, those by Hills and Ritchie, furnishing perhaps, the best idea of the picture. The military portrait has been well engraved by Kelly. The heads engraved by Gimbrede and Rawdon may be intended as from this picture, but if so, the intention has not been successfully carried out, particularly in the latter one.

177. ANDREWS.

WASHINGTON. Bust, head to left. Vignette. *Line.*

Height 4 12-16 inches; width 3 8-16 inches.

From the original painting by Stuart taken from life, in possession of the Boston Athenæum. Engraved by Joseph Andrews.

A fine example of pure line work, and one of this engraver's best efforts. It is a good rendering of the original. The plate engraved in 1843, was destroyed in the great Boston fire of 1872.

178. BAKER.

GENERAL WASHINGTON. Bust, head to left. Oval. *Line.*

Height 3 10-16 inches; width 2 12-16 inches.

Engraved by J. Baker. *Published May 10th 1800 by W. Bent.*

179. BALCH.

G. WASHINGTON. Bust, head to left. Vignette. *Line.*

Height 3 inches; width 2 10-16 inches.

Eng⁴ by V. Balch from a Painting by G. Stuart.

[The Presidents of the United States, Their Memories and Administrations. New York, 1850.]

180. BALLIN.

WASHINGTON. Full Bust in uniform, Head to left.   On the left breast, the order of the Cincinnati.   Vignette.   *Line.*

Height 3 12-16 inches; width 4 inches.

Ballin del. et sculp.   *Publié par Dufour, Mulat et Boulanger.   Imp. Gilquin et Dupain r. de la Calandre 19 Paris.*

A made up head, only slightly resembling Stuart.

181. BANK NOTE CO.

Bust, head to right.   Oval.   *Line.*

Height 3-16 inch; width 2-16 inch.

This is the smallest engraved Portrait of Washington.   The name of the Engraver, could not be ascertained.

182. BATHER.

G. WASHINGTON.   Full Bust, head to left.   Vignette.   *Stipple.*

Height 5 8-16 inches; width 4 8-16 inches.

Painted by G. Stuart.   Engraved by J. G. Bather Jr.

183. BAUMANN.

G. WASHINGTON,   Bust to right, Head turned to the left.   *Line.*

Height 4 8-16 inches; width 3 3-16 inches.

Dalla Libera.   I. W. Baumann sc^t. Mchn.

Later impressions, "Printed and published by G. L. Lange at Darmstadt."   A copy of the head by Longhi, No. 281.

184. BERTONNIER.

WASHINGTON. Bust, head to right. Inclosed by two slight lines, surmounted by a Globe, over which is an Eagle, beneath a star emitting rays; at the sides and bottom, beautifully engraved wreaths, Flags &c. &c. *Line.*

Height 2 4-16 inches; width 1 12-16 inches.

Bertonnier sculpt. "Galerie Napoleon." *Bernard Editeur Galerie Vivienne N°. 49.*

This plate, all the ornaments, lines &c. being removed, was published with the Title "Washington (George)," in the "Iconographie instructive." *Paris. De l'Imprimerie de Rignoux rue des Francs. Bourgeois S. Michel, No. 8.*

185. BEST.

G. WASHINGTON. Head to the right. Oval, with ruled background. *Line.*

Height 5 13-16 inches; width 5 inches.

Engraved expressly for Graham's Magazine from the original Painting by G. Stuart, by E. S. Best at J. M. Butler's establishment 84 Chestnut St.

186. BEST.

G. WASHINGTON. Head to the right. Oval, with ruled background. *Line.*

Height 3 inches; width 2 10-16 inches.

[Godey's Ladys Book.]

187. BURT.

Full Bust, head to right. *Line.*

Height 5 inches; width 3 12-16 inches.

Stuart Pinx^t. C. Burt sc.

[A Popular History of the United States. By William Cullen Bryant. Vol. III. New York, 1879. Also, "The Life and Works of Gilbert Stuart." By George C. Mason. New York, 1879.]

A fine and finished production, and an extremely close rendering of the original. Stuart's touch and handling are admirably given. From the " Gibbs Portrait," referred to in the text. This is the latest engraved Portrait of Washington.

188. BUTTRE.

G. WASHINGTON. Full Bust, head to left. Vignette. *Mezzotinto.*

Height 5 inches; width 4 4-16 inches.

Painted by G. Stuart. Engraved by J. C. Buttre.

189. BUTTRE.

G. WASHINGTON. Bust, head to left. Oval. *Mixed.*

Height 6 7-16 inches; width 5 4-16 inches.

G. Stuart. J. C. Buttre.

190. BUTTRE.

G. WASHINGTON. Bust, head to left. (Tea Pot Portrait.) Vignette. *Mixed.*

Height 3 12-16 inches; width 3 4-16 inches.

G. Stuart. J. C. Buttre.

[Life of General Washington. By John N. Norton, A. M. New York, 1860.]

191. BUTTRE.

GEORGE WASHINGTON. Full Bust, head to left. Oval, in a rectangle. In the angles, representations of scenes at Trenton, Princeton, Valley Forge, and Yorktown. *Mixed.*

Height 13 8-16 inches; width 10 2-16 inches.

Engraved and Published by J. C. Buttre 48 *Franklin St. New York.* (1866.) Border Designed by W. Mornberger.

192. CASILEAR.

Bust, head to left. The upper one, in an ornamented quarto sheet entititled, "The Presidents of the United States," containing portraits of Washington, John Adams, Jefferson, Madison, Monroe, John Quincy Adams and Andrew Jackson, in borders resembling picture frames, suspended on a wall. *Line.*

Height 2 3-16 inches; width 2 inches.

Designed by Robert W. Weir. Engraved by J. W. Casilear. From original and accurate portraits. Painted & engraved expressly for the New York Mirror. (Copy Right New York 1834.)

193. CHAPMAN.

GENERAL WASHINGTON. Bust in uniform, head to right. *Stipple.*

Height 4 8-16 inches; width 3 6-16 inches.

J. Chapman sc. *Published as the act directs Mar 1, 1800. Rare.*

Subsequently published without engraver's name, as " Engraved for the Encylopædia Londinensis 1828." A make up, based on the Stuart head.

194. CHORLEY.

GENERAL WASHINGTON. Full length, standing. The "Lansdowne Portrait." Fully described in the print by James Heath, No. 250.

Line.

Height 19 12-16 inches; width 13 inches.

Painted by Gilbert Stuart 1797. Engraved by John Chorley, Boston. *Printed by Pendleton Boston.*

195. CLARKE.

G. WASHINGTON, WHO DEPARTED THIS LIFE, DEC᙮ 14, 1799. AGED 68. Bust, head to left. Circle, in a rectangle engraved to represent stone work. The title beneath the circle. *Stipple.*

Height 2 10-16 inches; width 2 4-16 inches.

16

T. C. Clarke sc.   *Sold by W. Spotswood.*

[The United States Gazetteer.   By Joseph Scott.   Philadelphia, 1795.]

196. COIGNETO.

WASHINGTON (GEORGE).   Bust, head to right.   *Line.*

Height 2 4-16 inches; width 1 12-16 inches.

Melle Coigneto sc.   "Iconographie Instructive."

197. DALL 'ACQUA.

GIORGIO WASHINGTON.   Full Bust, head to right.   (Lansdowne.)
                                                              Line.
Height 5 inches; width 3 9-16 inches.

Stuart pin.   Dall 'Acqua inc.

198. DAVENPORT.

GENERAL WASHINGTON.   Full length, head to left.   The "Lansdowne Portrait."   Fully described in the print by James Heath, No. 250.   *Line.*

Height 4 inches; width 2 10-16 inches.

Davenport sculp.   *London Published by Thomas Tegg & Son Cheapside 1st Decr 1835.*

[The Life and Times of General Washington.   By Cyrus R. Edmonds.   London 1835.]

199. DELAISTRE.

WASHINGTON.   Bust, head to left.   (Lansdowne.)   Vignette.   *Etched.*

Height 3 8-16 inches; width 3 inches.

Vernier del.   Lemaitre dir.   Delaistre sc.

200. DODD.

Bust in uniform, head to right.   Vignette.   *Line.*

Height 2 inches; width 1 8-16 inches.

S. Dodd sc.   Newark.

Only one impression of this, has come under the notice of the writer.

201. DONEY.

WASHINGTON.   Three quarter length, sitting, a dress sword in left forearm; to the left, a table upon which is an inkstand, pen and upright book.   Oval, with border in a rectangle, ornamented corners.

Mezzotinto.

Height 12 10-16 inches; width 9 13-16 inches.

Painted by Stuart.   Engraved by Doney.   *Published by Rice & Allen corner of Burdick and Walter Sts. Kalamazoo Mich.*

From a picture painted by Stuart in 1822.

202. DONEY.

Bust, head to right.   *Mezzotinto.*

Height 4 12-16 inches; width 3 11-16 inches.

This plate a very poor effort, was never lettered.

203. DONEY.

WASHINGTON.   Three quarter length, head to left, the right hand on an upright book upon a table, the left upon the hilt of a dress sword held perpendicular.   The back of an arm chair partly visible to the right, and the background formed by a recess, with pillars on each side.   *Mezzotinto.*

Height 13 12-16 inches; width 10 12-16 inches.

Engraved by T. Doney.   (Copyright by Wm. Pate, 1865.)

A copy of the print by A. H. Ritchie after P. F. Rothermel, No. 312.

204. DOOLITTLE.

GEORGE WASHINGTON. Bust, head to right. Oval. *Stipple.*

Height 4 inches; width 3 7-16 inches.

A. Doolittle sc. "Connecticut Magazine." *Extremely rare.*

Only six numbers, of "The Connecticut Magazine or Gentleman's and Lady's Monthly Museum," published at Bridgeport, commencing January, 1801, and ending with the June number, were issued. This print is in the January number.

205. DUPRÉEL.

GEORGE WASHINGTON. Full Bust, head to right. (Lansdowne.)
Line.

Height 5 inches; width 3 11-16 inches.

Stuart pinx^t. Dupréel sc.

206. DURAND.

WASHINGTON. Full Bust, head to left. *Line.*

Height 4 9-16 inches; width 3 11-16 inches.

Painted by G. Stuart. Engraved by A. B. Durand. From the original picture in the possession of the Athenæum, Boston.

[The writings of George Washington. By Jared Sparks. Boston, 1834.]

Proofs have the artists' names "G. C. Stuart pt.," and "A. B. Durand sc.," traced with the point. One of the best engraved portraits of Washington. A well printed, early impression, conveys to the mind of the observer, a sense of excellence, and taste of execution, which is extremely pleasing and satisfactory.

207. EDWARDS.

WASHINGTON. Full Bust, head to left. Oval, with arabesque border; beneath, the representation of a battle. "Trenton." *Stipple.*

Height 8 inches; width 5 8-16 inches.

Stuart. Edwards. *London George Virtue.*

[The History of The United States of America. By W. H. Bartlett and B. B. Woodward, B.A. London and New York, 1856.]

208. EDWIN.

GEORGE WASHINGTON ESQ.ᴿ. Bust, head to left. Oval. *Stipple.*

Height 5 11-16 inches; width 4 8-16 inches.

Engraved from an original Picture by D. Edwin. T. B. Freeman Excudit. *Philadelphia Published by T. B. Freeman May 1ˢᵗ 1798.*

Extremely rare in this state.

The impressions of this plate usually seen, are those taken after it was entirely worked over, the address and " T. B. Freeman Excudit," having been erased. They are comparatively recent, lose much of the character of the original, and have the following inscription in three lines. " Born Feb'ʸ 22, 1732, took command of the American Army 1775, elected President of the United States April 30ᵗʰ 1789, resign'd 1796, Died Dec'ʳ 14ᵗʰ 1799," with the address of " I Scoles, New York."

209. EDWIN.

Bust, head to left. Oval. *Stipple.*

Height 4 14-16 inches; width 4 2-16 inches.

D. Edwin Fecit. *Philadelphia Published Jany 1ˢᵗ 1800 by A. Dickins.*

[George Washington to the People of the United States Announcing his Intention of Retiring from Public Life. Philadelphia, 1800.]

Also prefixed to " The Washingtoniana," Lancaster, 1802.

210. EDWIN.

GEO. WASHINGTON. Full Bust, head to left. *Stipple.*

Height 4 13-16 inches; width 4 inches.

D. Edwin sc.

[The Life of George Washington Commander in Chief of the American Forces, etc. etc. By John Marshall. Philadelphia, 1804.]

Edwin engraved several of these Plates, some of which are still in existence, in order to supply the demand for the work. The variations are scarcely noticeable.

211. EDWIN.

WASHINGTON. Full Bust, head to left. Ornamental border.

Stipple.

Height 8 inches; width 5 6-16 inches.

Philadᵃ Published by M A Milliette 320 Chestnut St.

The impressions usually seen, have the address, "Philadᵃ Published by Joseph Parker."

212. EDWIN.

GEORGE WASHINGTON GENERAL AND COMMANDER IN CHIEF OF THE AMERICAN REVOLUTIONARY ARMY AND FIRST PRESIDENT OF THE UNITED STATES. Bust, head to right. Oval.   ⁀   *Stipple.*

Height 4 inches; width 3 5-16 inches.

Edwin sc.

[An Essay on the Life of George Washington Commander in Chief etc. etc. By Aaron Bancroft, A. A. S. Worcester, 1807.]

213. EDWIN.

WASHINGTON, A NATIONS JOY. Full Bust, head to left. Oval.

Stipple.

Height 2 13-16 inches; width 2 2-16 inches.

Edwin sc.

[The Life of General George Washington. By John Kingston. Baltimore, 1813.]

214. EDWIN.

Bust, head to left. Oval. Above it a star, and the words "Centenary Anniversary;" beneath, "Feb. 22. 1832" and "We Perpetuate The Fine Arts." *Stipple.*

Height 2 8-16 inches; width 1 13-16 inches.

"Printed during the Procession by the Association of Copper-plate Printers." *Pub. by R. H. Hobson 147 Chest. St.*

This appears to be the preceding Plate, reduced. The Procession referred to, is the one which took place in Philadelphia Feby. 22. 1832, upon the occasion of the Centennial celebration, of the birthday of Washington.

215. EDWIN.

WASHINGTON. Bust, head to left.

> "Take him for all in all,
> We ne'er shall look upon his like again."

Vignette. *Stipple.*

Height 2 3-16 inches; width 1 4-16 inches.

Edwin sc. *Rare.*

[A collection of American Epitaphs and Inscriptions, with occasional Notes. By Rev. Timothy Alden, A. M. New York, 1814.]

216. EDWIN.

HIS EXCELLENCY GEORGE WASHINGTON Lieut GENl OF THE ARMIES OF THE UNITED STATES OF AMERICA. Three quarter length in uniform, sitting, the order of the Cincinnati on the left breast. A sword lies in the right fore-arm, and a chart in the hand, the left hand resting upon that portion of it which is upon a table. A curtain drawn up at the right, reveals an encampment in the distance. In the lower margin, an Eagle displayed, with shield and motto, "E Pluribus Unum."

Stipple.

Height 11 3-16 inches; width 8 10-16 inches.

F. Bartoli Pinxt. D. Edwin sc. "Respectfully Dedicated to the Lovers of their Country and Firm Supporters of Its Constitution."

No information could be obtained of this painter F. Bartoli. The picture may have been made up for the purpose of being engraved, the Stuart head or a resemblance to it, being introduced for the purpose of giving it popularity.

217. EDWIN.

WASHINGTON SACRED TO MEMORY. Three quarter length in uniform, seated. The same as the preceding plate, with the addition of a border 11-16 inches in width, the title in a tablet in the upper part. Beneath

the portrait and let into the border a funeral urn, supported by two female figures, and surrounded by war emblems.   Upon the top of the
urn, a sword and field glass crossed, and on a medallion, in three lines
"OB. Dec. 14, 1799. Æt. 68."   *Stipple.*

Height 11 3-16 inches; width 8 10-16 inches.

F. Bartoli pinx*. D. Edwin sc.   Revised by I. J. Barralet.   *Published by D. Kennedy 228 Market St. Philad*.*   *Rare.*

The only perceptible difference between the portrait of this, and the preceding print
is in the cuff on the right arm, which is not so wide.

218. EDWIN & MURRAY.

WASHINGTON.   Bust, head to left.   Oval medallion, the upper one of
a group of four, in an ornamented vignette.   The others, contain the
portraits of Adams, Jefferson, and Madison.   *Stipple.*

Height 2 inches; width 1 8-16 inches.

D. Edwin.   G. Murray.

[The History of the Reign of George III. to the Termination of the
late War.   By Robert Bisset L.L.D.   Philadelphia 1811.]

219. ENSOM.

GENERAL GEORGE WASHINGTON.   Bust, head to right.   *Line.*

Height 2 10-16 inches; width 2 inches.

Painted by Stuart.   Engraved by William Ensom.   *London Pub*d for
the Proprietor, September* 1822.

[Walmsley's Physiognomical Portraits.   London, 1824.]

220. FAIRMAN.

Bust, head to left.   Oval, with border, surrounded by diverging rays.
                                                        Stipple.

Height 5 8-16 inches; width 5 inches.

G. Stuart pinx*.   G. Fairman sculp*.

221. FAIRMAN.

WASHINGTON. Bust, head to left. Vignette.   *Stipple.*

Height 5 inches; width 4 8-16 inches.

Drawn by B. Trott from Stuart's picture. *Engraved and published by G. Fairman.*

Later impressions, "Fairman & Childs set."

222. FENNER, SEARS & CO.

GEORGE WASHINGTON. Half length, head to left. (Lansdowne.)
Line.

Height 7 7-16 inches; width 6 inches.

Engraved by Fenner, Sears & Co. from a painting by Stuart. *London Published May 2, 1831 by R. Ackerman 96 Strand, for the Proprietors of Hinton's History of America, 2 vols 4to Plates.*

This plate reduced to a full bust, and put into an oval with ornamented border, was subsequently published with the address, "J. & F. Tallis, London, Edinburgh, and Dublin."

223. FELSING.

GEORGIUS WASHINGTON. Bust to right, head to left.   *Line.*

Height 7 inches; width 5 inches.

G. Longhi dis. G. G. Felsing inc. *A Paris chez Tessari et Cie Rue du Cloitre Notre Dame No. 4.*

A remarkably close copy of the print by Longhi, No. 281, executed by Felsing at Milan in 1824, when a student under that engraver. The lettered impressions are the earliest, the title having been subsequently removed.

224. FERRIS.

Head to left. Vignette.   *Etched.*

Height 9 inches; width 7 4-16 inches.

17

225. FISHER.

GEORGE WASHINGTON ESQ^R. Half length, head to left. Background formed by a curtain, drawn up to the left, revealing a Pillar. (*Printed in colors.*) *Mezzotinto.*

Height 12 inches; width 10 inches.

Painted by C. G. Stuart. Engraved by James Fisher. From the original Picture in the possession of J. Sebⁿ De Franca Esqr of Devonshire Square London. *London Publish'd by P. Fische April 10th 1801. Extremely rare.*

226. FITTLER.

GEORGE WASHINGTON, First President of the United States of America. Full Bust, head to left. *Line.*

Height 5 8-16 inches; width 4 inches.

Stuart Pinx^t. Fittler sculpt. Engraved by James Fittler A. R. A. from the original picture painted by G. Stuart in the possession of the Most Noble the Marquis of Lansdown. *London, Published as the act directs May 15. 1804 by Richard Phillips, N° 71 St Pauls Church Yard.*

[Life of George Washington. By John Marshall. London, 1804.]

227. FREEMAN.

G. WASHINGTON. Half length, head to left. *Stipple.*

Height 4 8-16 inches; width 3 8-16 inches.

Engraved by S. Freeman from a painting by Stuart. *Rare.*

228. GALLAND.

HIS EXCELLENCY GEORGE WASHINGTON Lieu^t Genl of the Armies of the United States of America. Three quarter length in uniform, seated. In the lower margin, an Eagle displayed, with shield and motto, "E Pluribus Unum." (More fully described in the print by Edwin, No. 216.) *Stipple.*

Height 11 inches; width 8 10-16 inches.

F. Bartoli Pinx. J. Galland sculp. "Dedicated to Commodore John Barry and the Officers of the Navy and Army of North America."

This appears to be the same Plate as Edwin, No. 216, with parts worked over. In these impressions, however, the rosette on the hat lying upon the table to the right, is larger. No other print, bearing the name of this engraver, has come to the knowledge of the writer.

229. GEOFFROY.

GEORGE WASHINGTON. Bust, head to left. Vignette. *Stipple.*

Height 3 8-16 inches; width 3 4-16 inches.

Geoffroy. d'apres le tableau de Stuart.

[Washington Fondation de la Republique des Etats-unis d'Amerique. Vie de Washington &c &c traduit de l'Anglais de M. Jared Sparks par M. Guizot. Paris, 1851.]

230. GIMBER.

GEORGE WASHINGTON. Full length, standing. The "Tea-Pot Portrait." Fully described in the print by J. H. Hills, No. 252.

Mezzotinto.

Height 24 5-16 inches; width 16 7-16 inches.

G. Stuart pinxt. S. H. Gimber.

231. GIMBREDE.

Full Bust in uniform, head to right. The upper one, of a group of Portraits in ovals, in an oblong quarto sheet, of Washington, Adams, Jefferson and Madison, with a draped back-ground. Over the Washington, is a star containing thirteen lesser ones, and above it, the words "American Star." *Stipple.*

Height 4 inches; width 3 5-16 inches.

N. York Design'd, Engrav'd & Publish'd by Tho⁸ Gimbrede Jan⁷ 30ᵗʰ 1812. *Printed by Andᵗʷ Maverick.*

232. GIMBREDE.

GEN^L GEORGE WASHINGTON. Full Bust, head to left. *Stipple.*

Height 4 8-16 inches; width 3 13-16 inches.

Stuart pt. Gimbrede sc. "Eng^d for the Biography of American Heroes." *Pub. by John Low N. Y.*

[The Biography of the Principal American Military and Naval Heroes. By Thomas Wilson. New York, 1817.]

233. GIRARDET.

Full Bust, head to left. Oval.   *Mezzotinto.*

Height 9 4-16 inches; width 7 12-16 inches.

Portrait of Washington painted from life by Stuart. Engraved by Ed. Girardet.

234. GOBRECHT.

WASHINGTON. A NATION's JOY. Bust, head to left, on left breast, the order of the Cincinnati. Oval.   *Stipple.*

Height 2 13-16 inches; width 2 3-16 inches.

C. Gobrecht fe.   *Rare.*

[The New American Biographic Dictionary. By J. Kingston. Baltimore, 1810.]

235. GOBRECHT.

GEORGE WASHINGTON. Full Bust, head to left.   *Stipple.*

Height 7 3-16 inches; width 6 2-16 inches.

Drawn by B. Trott. Engraved by C. Gobrecht.

[The Cyclopedia or Universal Dictionary of Arts, Sciences and Literature. By Abraham Rees, D.D., F.R.S. 1st Am. Ed. Philadelphia, 1821.]

236. GOODMAN & PIGGOTT.

GENERAL WASHINGTON PRESIDENT OF THE UNITED STATES, BORN FEBRUARY 22ND 1732, DIED DECEMBER 14TH 1799. Full length, standing. The "Lansdowne Portrait." Fully described in the print by James Heath, No. 250. *Stipple.*

Height 19 14-16 inches; width 13 inches.

Painted by G. Stuart, 1797. Engraved by C. Goodman and R. Piggott. *Published by W. H. Morgan N° 114 Chesnut Street Philad°.*

237. HALL.

Full Bust, head to left. (Lansdowne.) *Mixed.*

Height 6 7-16 inches; width 4 11-16 inches.

From the full length portait painted by Gilbert Stuart in 1796 in the possession of Mrs. Pierrepont of Brooklyn Heights.

[Life of George Washington. By Washington Irving. New York, 1856–59.]

238. HALL.

Head to left. Vignette, with background ruled to a rectangle. *Stipple.*

Height 6 inches; width 4 11-16 inches.

G. Stuart. H. B. Hall. From the original picture in the Boston Athenæum taken from life in 1795. Engraved for Irving's Life of Washington. *G. P. Putnam & Co N. York.*

239. HALL.

Full Bust, head to left. Vignette. *Line.*

Height 3 12-16 inches; width 3 8-16 inches.

Eng^d by H. B. Hall from the original painting by Stuart.

240. HALL.

WASHINGTON.　Bust, head to left.　Vignette.　　　*Stipple.*

Height 4 4-16 inches; width 3 12-16 inches.

Eng^d by H. B. Hall after a Picture by Stuart.

241. HALL.

G. WASHINGTON.　Bust, head to left.　Vignette.　　*Etched.*

Height 4 inches; width 3 8-16 inches.

Etch^d by H. B. Hall from a Picture by Stuart. *Published by H. B. Hall & Sons* 13 *Barclay St. N. Y.*

242. HALL.

G. WASHINGTON.　Full Bust, head to left.　Oval, with scroll frame, in which are thirteen stars, surmounted by an eagle and surrounded by laurel.　At the bottom the U. S. shield and flags.　　*Stipple.*

Height 10 inches; width 7 12-16 inches.

Drawn & engraved by H. B. Hall from the original Head by Stuart in the Athenæum, Boston. *Published by W. Pate* 16 *Burling Slip. N. Y.*

243. HALL & PERINE.

WASHINGTON.　Full Bust, head to left.　Oval, with border in a rectangle.　　　　　　　　　　　　　　　　*Stipple.*

Height 12 5-16 inches; width 9 8-16 inches.

Engraved by H. B. Hall and G. E. Perine.　Painted by Gilbert Stuart. *Published by Geo. E. Perine* 10 *Courtlandt Street.*

244. HALL.

Bust, head to left.　Vignette.　　　　　　　　　　　*Stipple.*

Height 5 inches; width 4 inches.

G. Stuart.　G. R. Hall.　From the original Picture in the Boston Athenæum taken from life in 1795. *New York W. A. Townsend.*

[The Home of Washington and its Associations. By Benson J. Lossing. New York, 1859.]

245. HALL.

WASHINGTON. Head to left. Vignette, with background ruled to a rectangle. *Etched.*

Height 4 8-16 inches; width 4 inches.

Etched by Alice Hall, aged 18, 1866.

246. HALPIN.

WASHINGTON. Full length, standing. The "Tea-Pot Portrait." Fully described in the print by J. H. Hills, No. 252. *Mezzotinto.*

Height 24 inches; width 16 8-16 inches.

G. Stuart Pinxᵗ. Eng. by J. Halpin. From the original picture in the State House at Hartford, Connecticut. Presented to the subscribers of the Columbian Magazine, 1848. *New York Published By John S. Taylor 151 Nassau St.*

247. HARRISON.

WASHINGTON ÆTATIS 68. Bust, head to left. Oval. *Stipple.*

Height 2 12-16 inches; width 2 2-16 inches.

G. Stuart pinxᵗ. C. P. Harrison scult.

Only one impression of this, has come under the notice of the writer.

248. HARRISON.

Bust in uniform, head to left, the order of the Cincinnati on the right breast. Circle, surrounded by a wreath containing the names of twenty-three States, with diverging rays. A pen and sword crossed at the top. *Stipple.*

Diameter 1 3-16 inches.

G. Stewart pinx.   "Respectfully Dedicated to the Cincinnati Society."   *Design'd, Engrav'd, Printed & Published by C. P. Harrison
Feby 22^d.*

249. HATCH.

IORGE WASHINGTON.   Bust, head to left.   Vignette.   *Line.*

Height 3 4-16 inches; width 2 8-16 inches.

Painted by Stewart.   Engraved by Hatch.

Only one impression of this, has come under the notice of the writer.

250. HEATH.

GENERAL WASHINGTON.   Full length standing, head to left.   The
right arm is extended as if speaking, and a dress sword in the left hand,
is held by his side.   To the left, a table partly covered with a cloth,
upon which an inkstand and books; beneath the table, are also some
books.   To the right, a little in the rear, an arm chair, and in the background two rows of pillars, between which, is a curtain partly drawn up.
Line.
Height 19 13-16 inches; width 13 inches.

Painted by Gabriel Stuart 1797.   Engraved by James Heath Histori-
cal Engraver to his Majesty, and to his Royal Highness the Prince of
Wales, from the original Picture in the collection of the Marquis of
Lansdowne.   *Published Feby 1. 1800 by Ja^s Heath N° 42 Newman
Street, Messrs Boydells, Cheapside & J. P. Thomson Great Newport
Street London.*   Copy Right secured in the United States according to
Law.

Known as the "Lansdowne Portrait."   An Impression from the unfinished Plate,
the Title in open letters, without the artist's names, has come under the notice of the
writer.   It has the following address, " Published Octr 12. 1797 by J. Heath N° 42
Newman Street & Messrs Robinson's Pater-Noster Row."   The statement frequently
made, that the error in lettering the Plate, "*Gabriel*," instead of *Gilbert* Stuart, was
subsequently corrected, is not founded on fact.   No impressions are known with such
alteration.

251. HEATH.

GENERAL WASHINGTON. Bust, head to left. (Lansdowne.) Oval.
Stipple.

Height 3 12-16 inches; width 3 inches.

Engrav'd by J. Heath from an original Picture by Stewart. *Publish'd Octr. 16. 1807, by Cadell & Davies, Strand, London.*

[The Life of George Washington, Commander in Chief, &c. By David Ramsay, M.D. London, 1807.]

252. HILLS.

WASHINGTON. Full length standing, the right hand resting by the fingers, upon a table to the left. In the left hand, a dress sword held at the side. The coat is drawn together by a single upper button. In the rear, to the right, an arm chair. *Line.*

Height 20 2-16 inches; length 14 4-16 inches.

Painted by G. Stuart. Engraved by J. H. Hills.

Known as the "Tea Pot Portrait," from the position of the arms. The figure is fuller and turned more to the left, than in the "Lansdowne," and is much better drawn. The accessories are the same.

253. HILLS.

Full length. The "Lansdowne Portrait." *Line.*

Height 2 7-16 inches; width 1 9 16 inches.

J. H. Hills sc.

254. HINCHLIFF.

GENERAL WASHINGTON. Full Bust in uniform, head to left.
Line.

Height 4 inches; width 3 14-16 inches.

Stewart. Hinchliff.

18

255. HOLL.

GENERAL WASHINGTON. Bust, head to right. Oval. *Stipple.*

Height 2 inches; width 1 8-16 inches.

Hall sculp.

[Biographical Magazine containing Portraits with Lives and Characters of eminent Persons. London, n. d.]

256. HOLL.

GEORGE WASHINGTON First President of the United States of America. Full Bust, head to left. (Lansdowne.) *Stipple.*

Height 5 2-16 inches; width 4 inches.

G. Stuart Pinxt. W. Holl sculp. *Published by Edwd Barnes, Leeds Nov.* 1. 1821.

257. HOLL.

GEO. WASHINGTON. Full Bust, head to left. In a frame, draped and resting upon a Base, with army and navy emblems at the sides. At the top, a bust of Minerva (helmeted), between the figures of a soldier and sailor. *Stipple.*

Height 6 12-16 inches; width 4 4-16 inches.

Painted by C. G. Stuart. Engraved by W. Holl. *London Published by Thomas Kelly* 17 *Paternoster Row April* 1830.

Later impressions, are without the border, base, and ornaments; the date, omitted from the address.

258. HOLLOWAY.

GEORGE WASHINGTON. Full Bust, head to right. *Line.*

Height 9 2-16 inches; width 7 12-16 inches.

Engraved by T. Holloway from a Picture painted by Mr Stuart in 1795 in the possession of Samuel Vaughan Esqr. *Published as the act directs by T. Holloway and the other Proprietors Nov^r* 2. 1796.

[Essays on Physiognomy. By John Caspar Lavater, Translated by Henry Hunter, D.D. London, 1789-98.]

The earliest engraving of Stuart's first portrait of Washington, known from its ownership as the "Vaughan Portrait." In referring to it in the text, the name of the engraver was given through inadvertence, as S. Holloway instead of T. Holloway.

259. HUMPHREYS.

WASHINGTON. Full Bust, head to left. *Stipple.*

Height 5 inches; width 4 inches.

Engraved by W. Humphreys. From a Picture by Gilbert Stewart in the possession of T. B. Barclay Esqr. of Liverpool. Under the Superintendence of the Society for the Diffusion of useful Knowledge. *London Published by Charles Knight, Ludgate Street.*

[The Gallery of Portraits with Memoirs. London, 1833-37.]

260. ILLMAN.

GEORGE WASHINGTON. Bust, head to left. Vignette. *Stipple.*

Height 2 6-16 inches; width 2 4-16 inches.

Drawn by Hoppner Meyer from the painting by G. Stuart. Engraved by T. Illman. *Entered according to Act of Congress in the District Court N. Y.*

261. ILLMAN & PILBROW.

GEORGE WASHINGTON. Full length. The "Tea Pot Portrait." Fully described in the print by J. H. Hills, No. 252. *Mezzotinto.*

Height 25 6-16 inches; width 16 12-16 inches.

Copied by permission from a painting by Stuart in the State House, Hartford, Conn. *Engraved & Published by Illman & Pilbrow New York.*

262. ILLMAN & PILBROW.

WASHINGTON. Full Bust, head to left. In the lower margin, a figure of Liberty seated, with eagle and shield. *Line.*

Height 8 14-16 inches; width 7 6-16 inches.

Painted by Stewart. Engraved by Illman & Pilbrow.

263. ILLMAN & CO.

GEORGE WASHINGTON. Full length. The "Tea Pot Portrait."
Fully described in the print by J. H. Hills, No. 252.   *Line.*

Height 6 inches; width 4 inches.

Stuart pinxt.   Engᵈ by Illman & Co.

264. ILLMAN & SON.

Head to left.   Oval, with narrow scroll border.   Heading to an imperial
folio sheet, entitled "The Declaration of Independence and Portraits
of the Presidents."   *Stipple.*

Height 3 inches; width 2 6-16 inches.

Engraved and printed by Illman & Son, 603 Arch St. Philadᵃ. "Led-
ger Carriers' Annual Greeting to Their Subscribers 1859."

265. JOCELYN.

GEN. WASHINGTON. ONE OF THE FEW WHO HAVE BEEN GREAT WITHOUT
BEING CRIMINAL, WAS A NATIVE OF VIRGINIA, BORN 1731, TOOK COM-
MAND OF THE AMERICAN ARMY AT BOSTON 1775, RESIGNED HIS COM-
MAND 1783, WAS INAUGURATED PRESIDENT OF THE UNITED STATES
1789; AND AGAIN 1793; AND DIED 1799. Full Bust, head to left.
(Lansdowne.)   *Line.*

Height 3 12-16 inches; width 3 inches.

Stuart pinxt.   S. S. Jocelyn sculpt.

266. JOHNSTON.

GEORGE WASHINGTON. Bust, head to right.   Vignette.   *Stipple.*

Height 3 inches; width 2 inches.

D. C. Johnston sc.

[The Life of George Washington, First President of the United
States. By Aaron Bancroft, D.D. Boston, 1826.]

267. KELLY.

WASHINGTON. Full length in uniform, left hand holding the bridle, and resting upon the saddle of a horse to the right, fore-shortened. In his right hand, by his side, a large chapeau. In the left distance, shipping, smoke, etc. *Line.*

Height 23 10-16 inches; width 15 14-16 inches.

From a copy by M. A. Swett taken from the original picture by Stuart in Faneuil Hall. Painted by Gilbert Stuart. Engraved by T. Kelly. "Entered according to the Act of Congress in the year 1836 by L. P. Clover in the Clerk's Office of the District Court of the Southern District of New York." *Printed by A. King.*

Later impressions, "Published by the Franklin Print Company 46 Court St. Boston." *Printed by K. Neale.* The picture represents Washington at Dorchester Heights.

268. KELLY.

G. WASHINGTON. Full Bust, head to left. *Stipple.*

Height 4 9-16 inches; width 3 12-16 inches.

Painted by Stuart. Engraved by T. Kelly. *Published by Samuel Walker (Harlem Place) Washington Street Boston.*

269. KENNEDY.

GEN^L GEORGE WASHINGTON. Half length, head to left.
Mezzotinto.

Height 16 2-16 inches; width 13 12-16 inches.

J. Kennedy sct. Engraved from the original Picture Painted by Gabriel Stewart Esqr Now in the possession of Paul Beck Esqr. "This print is respectfully Dedicated to the citizens of the United States by T. W. Freeman." Freeman Excudit. *Printed & Published by T. W. Freeman Philadelphia 1st Sept. 1813.* *Rare.*

Also printed in colors.

270. KIMBERLY.

GEORGE WASHINGTON. Full length. The "'Tea Pot Portrait.'' Fully described in the Print by J. H. Hills, No. 252. Arched top. The centre of a folio sheet, entitled "The Presidents of the United States," and surrounded by nine oval medallions, containing portraits of John Adams, Thomas Jefferson, James Madison, James Monroe, John Quincy Adams, Andrew Jackson, Martin Van Buren, William Henry Harrison and John Tyler.   *Line.*

Height 6 12-16 inches; width 4 14-16 inches.

G. Stuart del. Designed by C. H. H. Billings. Engraved by D. Kimberly. *Published by Charles A. Wakefield N° 56 Cornhill Boston.* (1842.)

271. KIRKWOOD.

GENERAL WASHINGTON. Bust, head to right. (Lansdowne.)
Line.

Height 3 inches; width 2 8-16 inches.

Eng^d by Kirkwood & Son.

272. KNEASS.

WASHINGTON. Full Bust, head to left.   *Stipple.*

Height 4 3-16 inches; width 3 7-16 inches.

W. Kneass sc. Philad^a. *Published by J. Downing, Lexington Kent^y.*

273. LAWSON.

G. WASHINGTON. Bust, head to left. Oval, with border in a rectangle; beneath the oval upon a base, a helmet, sword and baton, with oak and laurel branches.   *Line.*

Height 6 7-16 inches; width 4 inches.

Baralet Dirext. Lawson sc. *Published by R. Campbell & Co.* From a copy painted by J. Paul.

[Continuation of Mr. Hume's History, By a Society of Gentlemen. Philadelphia, 1798.]

Later impressions have the address of " Conrad and Co."

274. LENEY.

GEO. WASHINGTON.   Full Bust, head to left.   *Stipple.*

Height 4 inches; width 3 4-16 inches.

Leney set. N. Y.

[The Life of George Washington, Commander in chief of the Armies of the United States of America, &c. &c.   By David Ramsay, M.D.   New York, 1807.]

275. LENEY.

WASHINGTON.   Full Bust, head to left.   *Stipple.*

Height 3 8-16 inches; width 2 14-16 inches.

Stuart pinxt.   Leney set.   Engrav'd for the Washington Benevolent Society in the city of New York.

[Washington's Farewell Address to the People of the United States. Published for the Washington Benevolent Society, New York, 1808.]

276. LENEY.

GEO. WASHINGTON.   Full Bust, head to left.   *Stipple.*

Height 3 8-16 inches; width 2 14-16 inches.

Leney sc. N. Y.   Engrav'd for the Washington Benevolent Society.

[Washington's Farewell Address to the People of the United States. Published for the Washington Benevolent Society of Cranberry.   New Brunswick, 1812.]

A different plate from the preceding one.

277. LONGACRE.

GEORGE WASHINGTON. Bust, head to left. Circular medallion, the heading to a sheet 33 by 24 inches, containing "The Declaration of Independence," surrounded by fifteen others, two of which, contain portraits of Jefferson and Hancock, and the remainder, the coats of arms of the thirteen original States.   *Stipple.*

Diameter 5 inches.

"Entered according to Act of Congress the 4th day of November 1818 by John Binns of the State of Pennsylvania."

278. LONGACRE.

GEORGE WASHINGTON. Bust, head to left. Vignette.   *Stipple.*

Height 4 inches; width 4 inches.

Engraved by J. B. Longacre from a miniature by M[r] Trott.

[The Cyclopedia or Universal Dictionary of Arts, Sciences and Literature. By Abraham Rees, D.D. F.R.S. 1st Am. Ed. Philadelphia —1821.]

279. LONGACRE.

WASHINGTON. Bust, head to left. Ornamented border.   *Stipple.*

Height 4 10-16 inches; width 2 12-16 inches.

Painted by Stuart. Engraved by J. B. Longacre. *C. S. Williams New Haven Ct.*

280. LONGACRE.

WASHINGTON. Full Bust, head to left.   *Stipple.*

Height 4 4-16 inches; width 3 6-16 inches.

Engraved by J. B. Longacre from a painting by G. Stuart.

[The National Portrait Gallery of Distinguished Americans. Philadelphia 1834.]

281. LONGHI.

GEORGIUS WASHINGTON.   Bust to right, head to left.   *Line.*

Height 7 inches; width 5 inches.

G⁰ Longhi dis. ed inc. per Dalla Libera.

[Vite e Ritratti di cento uomini illustri.   Bettoni.   Padua.]

Engraved in 1817 from a drawing made by Longhi himself, the Stuart and Trumbull heads, probably, being combined.   The hair, executed after the manner of Masson, in his celebrated print of "Guillaume de Brisacier," known as the *Gray-headed Man*, engraved in 1664, is thoroughly artificial, and while showing great dexterity on the part of the engraver, removes it still further from any original.

282. —— ——.

GEORGES WASHINGTON, PREMIER PRESIDENT DES ETATS-UNIS D'AMERIQUE, NÉ LE 22 FEVRIER 1732, DANS LE COMTÉ DE WESTMORLAND, EN VIRGINIE, MORT À MOUNT VERNON LE 15 NOVᵇᴿᴿ 1799.   Bust to right, head to the left.   Circle in a squared plate.   *Stipple.*

Diameter 5 6-16 inches.

A Paris chez l'auteur, Rue des Francs Bourgeois N° 6, F. Sᵗ. Gᵐ.

A copy of the preceding print.

283. —— ——.

WASHINGTON (GEORGES), NÉ A WASHINGTON LE 11 FEVRIER 1732, MORT LE 14 DECEMBRE 1799.   Bust to right, head turned to the left.   Vignette.   *Line.*

Height 2 13-16 inches; width 2 6-16 inches.

Publié par Blaisot.

A copy of the print by Longhi, No. 281.

19

284. MACKENZIE.

GEO^E WASHINGTON Esq^R LATE PRESIDENT & COMMANDER IN CHIEF OF THE FORCES OF THE UNITED STATES OF AMERICA. Full Bust, head to right. Oval. *Stipple.*

Height 3 13-16 inches; width 3 inches.

Engraved by K. Mackenzie from an original Picture. *London, Published by G. Cawthorn, British Library* 152 *Strand.*

285. MACRET.

GEORGE WASHINGTON. Full Bust, head to left. (Lansdowne.)
Stipple.

Height 3 8-16 inches; width 2 10-16 inches.

Gravé par Macret, rue des Fossés M. le Prince N° 18.

[Vie de Georges Washington, General en Chef des Armées des Etats Unis pendant la guerre qui á établi leur independence, et prémiere President des Etats Unis, par David Ramsay. Paris, 1809.]

286. MARSHALL.

G. WASHINGTON. Full Bust, head to left. Oval, with border in a rectangle. *Line.*

Height 13 8-16 inches; width 11 4-16 inches.

Engraved by William E. Marshall From the original Portrait in the Boston Athenæum. Painted by Gilbert Stuart. *Published November* 15*th* 1862, *By Ticknor and Fields,* 135 *Washington St. Boston. Copyright secured.*

Marshall's Washington, has an established reputation, and occupies as an engraving, in the popular mind, the same relative position, which the original does as a painting.

287. MAVERICK.

WASHINGTON. Bust, head to left. Oval medallion, surrounded by war emblems, and to the right another, containing a portrait of Lafayette. *Line.*

Height 1 12-16 inches; width 1 6-16 inches.

Peter Maverick sc.

288. MAYER.

GEORGE WASHINGTON. Half length, head to left. (Lansdowne.)
Line.

Height 5 inches; width 3 14-16 inches.

Nach dem Gemalde im capitol. Mayer sculpsit. *Eigenthum & Verlag Des. Bibl. Instituts in Hildburghausen.*

Later impressions, have the title " Washington," and *Aus der Kunstanst des Bibliogr. Instit. in Hildbghsn.*

289. MAYER.

WASHINGTON. Bust, head to right. Vignette. *Line.*

Height 3 4-16 inches; width 3 8 16 inches.

Stahlstich von Carl Mayer. *Rare.*

290. McCARTY.

WASHINGTON. Bust, head to left. Vignette. *Line.*

Height 3 4-16 inches; width 2 12-16 inches.

McCarty sculpsit.

291. McRAE.

GEORGE WASHINGTON. Full Bust, head to left. *Stipple.*

Height 11 3-16 inches; width 9 10-16 inches.

Engraved and Published by John C. McRae, 100 Liberty St. New York.

292. MORSE.

Full Bust, head to left. Vignette. *Line.*

Height 3 12-16 inches; width 3 2-16 inches.

Morse sc.

[Le General Washington et Madame la Generale. Biographies par M. Etourneau. Paris, 1860.]

293. NESMITH.

WASHINGTON. Full length. The "Lansdowne Portrait." Fully described in the print by James Heath, No. 250. *Line.*

Height 5 5-16 inches; width 3 9-16 inches.

Engraved by J. H. Nesmith. *Published by Hezekiah Howe and Darrie & Peck, New Haven Conn.*

[A Political and Civil History of the United States of America from 1763 to March 1797. By Timothy Pitkin. New Haven, 1828.]

294. NUTTER.

GEO. WASHINGTON Esqʀ, Late President of the United States of America. Full Bust, head to left. *Stipple.*

Height 8 14-16 inches; width 7 7-16 inches.

C. G. Stuart pinxt. W. Nutter sculpt. From an original Picture in the Possession of J. Sebⁿ De Franca Esqʳ of Devonshire Place to whom this Plate is Dedicated by his obliged humble Servᵗ Robᵗ Cribb. *London, Published Janʸ 15ᵗʰ 1798 by R. Cribb, Holborn.* *Rare.*

This was also printed in colors.

295. NUTTER.

GEORGE WASHINGTON Esqʀ, Late President of the United States of America. Full Bust, head to left. Oval. *Stipple.*

Height 5 2-16 inches; width 4 2-16 inches.

C. G. Stuart pinxt. W. Nutter sculpt. *London published by R. Cribb Janʸ 15, 1799.* *Very Rare.*

296. ORMSBY.

WASHINGTON. Half length, head to left. (Lansdowne.) *Line.*

Height 7 7-16 inches; width 6 2-16 inches.

W. L. Ormsby sc. *Boston Published by S. Walker.*

[The History and Topography of The United States of North America, &c. By John Howard Hinton, A.M. 1ˢᵗ Am. Ed. Boston, 1834.]

297. ORMSBY.

WASHINGTON. Full length. The "Lansdowne Portrait." Fully described in the Print by James Heath, No. 250. *Line.*

Height 20 2-16 inches; width 13 inches.

Painted by Gilbert Stuart. Eng'd on steel by W. L. Ormsby N. Y. *Published by W. L. Ormsby* 116 *Fulton Street N. Y.*

298. PARADISE.

PATRIÆ PATER. Bust, head to left. Oval. On left of oval, "Born Feb. 22d, 1732," on the right, "Died Dec. 14ᵗʰ 1799." *Line.*

Height 3 4-16 inches; width 2 12-16 inches.

Painted by G. C. Stuart. Eng. by J. W. Paradise.

299. PEABODY.

GEO. WASHINGTON. Bust, head to left. Oval. *Stipple.*

Height 2 inches; width 1 10-16 inches.

Peabody sc.

300. PEKENINO.

WASHINGTON. Bust, head to left. Border resembling a picture frame, suspended by a ring. *Stipple.*

Height 5 2-16 inches; width 4 6-16 inches.

Engraved by Mᵈˡ Pekenino Philadelphia 1822. From an original Portrait by G. Stewart.

301. PELTON.

WASHINGTON. Full length. The "Lansdowne Portrait." Fully described in the Print by James Heath, No. 250.   *Line.*

Height 20 inches; width 13 inches.

Painted by Gilbert Stuart. Engraved by O. Pelton. *Published by E. R. Pelton, Office of Eclectic Magazine No. 5 Beekman St. N. Y.*

302. PERINE.

GEORGE WASHINGTON. Full Bust, head to left. Oval.
Mezzotinto.

Height 8 3-16 inches; width 6 3-16 inches.

Eng^d by Geo. E. Perine. *Published by Moore & Co. 111 Nassau Street New York.*

303. PERINE.

WASHINGTON. Bust, slightly to left, head to right. Vignette.
Stipple.

Height 3 12-16 inches; width 3 6-16 inches.

Engraved by Geo. E. Perine N. York.

Copy of the Print by Longhi, No. 281.

304. PERKINS & HEATH.

WASHINGTON. Bust, head to left. Inclosed by a square border of lathe work, with a star in each corner. In the upper margin, an Eagle displayed, with U. S. shield and motto, "E. Pluribus Unum." In lower margin a flag, (upon which is the title,) rolled about a staff.

Height 2 13-16 inches; width 2 4-16 inches.

Perkins & Heath, Patent Hardened Steel Plate.   *Very rare.*

305. PERKINS.

Bust, head to left. Oval, with border of lathe work.   *Line.*

Height 1 inch; width 15-16 inch.

Centre of an oblong quarto sheet of ornamental Penmanship, entitled, "Sacred to the Memory of General Geo. Washington, The Father of His Country was born Feb. 22, 1732, Died Dec. 13, 1799."

Written and Engraved by Jos. Perkins New York 1826.

[The American Penman. By Perkins & Rand, Philadelphia. Published August, 1827.]

306. PORTMAN.

GEORGE WASHINGTON. Full Bust, head to left. (Lansdowne.) Oval. *Stipple.*

Height 4 6-16 inches; width 3 10-16 inches.

Stuart del. ad viv. L. Portman sc. *A. Loosjes Pz. exc.* 1805.

Rare.

307. RAWDON.

GEN. GEORGE WASHINGTON. Full Bust, in uniform, head to right.
Stipple.

Height 11 4-16 inches; width 9 inches.

Engraved by Ralph Rawdon. *Published & Sold by Shelton & Kensett, Cheshire Con. Jan. 16th 1814.*

Only one impression of this, has come under the notice of the writer. It is quite rude in the execution.

308. REED.

Bust, head to left. Vignette. Over the head, the figure of Fame with a trumpet and laurel wreath and the words "Pro Patria." Beneath the Bust, "Washington Benevolent Society." *Stipple.*

Height 2 8-16 inches; width 1 8-16 inches.

A. Reed sc. E. W. con. *Rare.*

[Biographical Memoirs of the Illustrious Gen. George Washington, Late President of the United States of America, &c. Barnard, Vt. 1813.]

309. RICE.

G. WASHINGTON. Full length. The "Lansdowne Portrait." Fully described in the Print by James Heath, No. 250.   *Mezzotinto.*

Height 19 14-16 inches; width 13 4-16 inches.

Painted by G. Stuart. Engraved by J. R. Rice.   *Published by Pohlig & Rice Philadelphia.*

310. RICE.

G. WASHINGTON. Full length. The "Lansdowne Portrait."
Mezzotinto.
Height 11 3-16 inches; width 7 10-16 inches.

Engraved by E. A. Rice.   *Smith & Holden Publishers, 82 West Baltimore St. Baltimore Md.*

311. RIDLEY.

GENERAL WASHINGTON. Full Bust, head to right.   Oval.
Stipple.
Height 4 inches; width 3 8-16 inches.

Engraved by W. Ridley, from an Original Picture in the possession of Saml Vaughan, Esqr. "European Magazine."   *Published by J. Sewell 32 Cornhill, April 1st 1800.*

312. RITCHIE.

G. WASHINGTON. Full length standing, head to left, right hand on an upright book upon a table to the left.   The left hand upon the hilt of a dress sword, the point on the ground.   The background formed by an alcove and pillars, and in the rear, to the right an arm chair.
Mezzotinto.
Height 26 6-16 inches; width 19 10-16 inches.

P. F. Rothermel pinxt.   A. H. Ritchie sc.   *Published by R. A. Bachia & Co. 23 Chambers St. N. Y.*   (Copy Right 1852.)

A copy of the full lengths, varied as described.

313. RITCHIE.

G. WASHINGTON. Full length. The "Tea Pot Portrait." Fully described in the print by J. H. Hills, No. 252. *Mezzotinto.*

Height 11 8-16 inches; width 7 12-16 inches.

Painted by Gilbert Stuart. Engraved by A. H. Ritchie. (Private Plate.)

[Washington's Farewell Address to the People of the United States of America. Reprint from the original MS. in the possession of James Lenox. Privately printed. New York, 1850.]

314. ROBERTS.

Bust, head to left. Oval. *Stipple.*

Height 3 2-16 inches; width 2 8-16 inches.

This plate was left unfinished, but not destroyed, as stated by Dunlap in his sketch of the engraver of it, John Roberts (Arts of Design, vol. i. 427). The impressions usually seen, are those taken about twenty years since.

315. ROBERTS.

GENERAL WASHINGTON. BORN FEB^Y 11TH 1732. DIED DEC. 14TH 1799. Head to left. Circular. *Stipple.*

Diameter 2 2-16 inches.

Roberts sc. *London, Published by C. Miller Old Fish S! S! Pauls.*

Only one impression of this, has come under the notice of the writer. It is printed on satin, forming one side of a pocket pincushion, the head of Franklin being on the other. The head almost fills the circle.

316. ROGERS.

GEORGE WASHINGTON. Nearly full length. (Lansdowne.)
Mixed.

Height 5 7-16 inches; width 3 13 16 inches.

20

J. Rogers sc. 381 B. W. *New York D. Appleton & Co.*

[Memoirs of Washington. By Mrs. C. M. Kirkland. New York, 1869.]

317. ROSMÄSTER.

GEORGE WASHINGTON, Präsident der Vereinigten Staaten von Amerika. Bust, head to left. (Lansdowne.) Oval. *Stipple.*

Height 5 7-16 inches; width 4 inches.

Rosmäster sculp.

318. RUSSEL.

WASHINGTON. Half length, head to left. A battle, indistinctly expressed in the background. Vignette. *Stipple.*

Height 4 12-16 inches.

Russel sculp. *London, Published (For the Proprietors) by John Saunders, 25 Newgate Street* 1835. *Rare.*

[Memoirs of the late William Cobbett, Esq'. By Robert Huish. London, 1836.]

319. SADD.

G. WASHINGTON. Full length. The "Lansdowne Portrait." Fully described in the print by James Heath, No. 250. *Mezzotinto.*

Height 20 4-16 inches; width 16 inches.

Painted by G. Stuart. Engraved by H. S. Sadd.

320. SADD.

WASHINGTON. Full length in uniform. "Washington at Dorchester Heights." Fully described in the print by T. Kelly, No. 267.

Mezzotinto.

Height 10 14-16 inches; width 7 10-16 inches.

G. Stuart P. On steel by H. S. Sadd. From the celebrated picture in Faneuil Hall, Boston. *Printed by Burton.*

321. SARTAIN.

GEORGE WASHINGTON. Bust, head to left. *Mezzotinto.*

Height 5 12-16 inches; width 4 12-16 inches.

The original by G. Stuart. Engraved by J. Sartain. *Published by*
R. R. Landon Ag', 88 Lake S' Chicago Ill.

322. SARTAIN.

G. WASHINGTON. Full Bust, head to left. Vignette. *Mezzotinto.*

Height 4 8-16 inches; width 4 inches.

Engraved by J. Sartain.

[Letters on Agriculture from His Excellency George Washington,
&c. to Arthur Young, Esqr. F.R.S. and Sir John Sinclair, Bart., M.P.
Edited by Franklin Knight. Washington, 1847.]

323. SARTAIN.

G. WASHINGTON. Full length. The "Tea Pot Portrait." Fully described in the print by J. H. Hills, No. 252. *Mezzotinto.*

Height 11 4-16 inches; width 7 4-16 inches.

Engraved by John Sartain. The original Picture by Gilbert Stuart.
(Private Plate.)

[Washington's Farewell Address to the People of the United States
of America. Reprint from the original MS. in the possession of James
Lenox. Privately printed. New York, 1850.]

324. SARTAIN.

WASHINGTON. Full length. The "Tea Pot Portrait." *Mezzotinto.*

Height 6 9-16 inches; width 5 inches.

Painted by G. Stuart. Engraved by J. Sartain. *J. L. White Phila".*

[Recollections and Private Memoirs of Washington. By G. W. P.
Custis. Philadelphia, 1861.]

325. SARTAIN.

GEORGE WASHINGTON.   Bust, head to right.   Oval, in a rectangle.
Mezzotinto.

Height 10 8-16 inches; width 8 12-16 inches.

Painted by Stuart. Engraved by John Sartain. Bradley & Co. Publishers 66 Nth 4ᵗʰ St. Philadelphia. (Copyright 1865.)

326. SARTAIN.

GEORGE WASHINGTON.   Full Bust, head to right.   Oval, in a rectangle.   *Mezzotinto.*

Height 11 2-16 inches ; width 9 6-16 inches.

Engraved & Published by William Sartain 728 Sansom St. Philadᵃ.

327. SCOLES.

Genᴸ GEORGE WASHINGTON departed this Life Decᴿ 14ᵀᴴ 1799, aged 68. Bust, head to right. Oval, in a rectangle. The title &c. in a tablet with arched top, beneath the oval.   *Stipple.*

Height 4 4-16 inches; width 2 14-16 inches.

Scoles sc.   *Publish'd by I. Low N. York.*   *Rare.*

[The Life of George Washington Commander in Chief of the Armies and late President of the United States of America. By John Corry. 1ˢᵗ Am. Ed. New York, 1807.]

328. SCOLES.

Genᴸ WASHINGTON. Born Feb. 22, 1732. Died Dec. 14, 1799. Bust, head to left. Oval.   *Stipple.*

Height 2 10-16 inches; width 2 2-16 inches.

Published by M. Carey.   *Rare.*

[The Life of George Washington with curious Anecdotes &c &c. By M. L. Weems. Philadelphia, 1808.]

329. SCOLES.

GEORGE WASHINGTON. Bust, head to left. Oval. *Stipple.*

Height 2 11-16 inches; width 2 3-16 inches.

Scoles sculp.

[The Life of George Washington First President and Commander in Chief of the United States of America. By John Corry. New York, 1809.]

330. SCOLES.

GEORGE WASHINGTON. Bust, head to left. Oval. *Stipple.*

Height 2 11-16 inches; width 2 3-16 inches.

[Life of Gen. George Washington late President of the United States of America and Commander in Chief of their Armies during the Revolutionary War. New York, 1825.]

A different Plate from the preceding one.

331. SMITH.

GEN^L GEORGE WASHINGTON. Bust, head to left. Oval. *Stipple.*

Height 2 12-16 inches; width 2 4-16 inches.

J. R. Smith Boston.

[Washington's Farewell Address to the People of the United States, together with the Constitution of the U. S. with all its amendments &c &c. Worcester, Mass. Printed by Isaac Sturtevant, 1813.]

This Plate is still in existence. Early impressions are rare.

332. SMITH.

G. WASHINGTON. Head to left. Oval, in a rectangle. *Stipple.*

Height 8 4-16 inches; width 6 10-16 inches.

Engraved by H. W. Smith from the original by Stuart in possession of the Boston Athenæum. Entered according to act of Congress in the year 1860 by S. Walker, Jr. in the Clerks Office of the District Court of Mass. *James Walker, Boston.*

333. SMITH.

G. WASHINGTON. Head to left. Vignette, with a background ruled to a rectangle. *Stipple.*

Height 7 11-16 inches; width 5 14-16 inches.

G. Stuart Pinxt. H. W. Smith N. Y.

334. SMITH.

G. WASHINGTON. Head to left. Vignette, with a background ruled to a rectangle. *Stipple.*

Height 12 8-16 inches; width 9 12-16 inches.

Engraved by H. Wright Smith after the Portrait by Stuart. Copyright, W. S. Baker. *Published By Lindsay & Baker, Philadelphia* 1879.

An excellent translation of the "Athenæum Head." The engraver seems to have caught the spirit of the original, and truly given us the motive of the Painter.

335. SOPER.

GEORGE WASHINGTON L. L. D. (1790). Bust, head to left. Oval. *Stipple.*

Height 3 8-16 inches; width 3 inches.

G. Stuart. R. Soper. *Published by J. C. Buttre N. Y.*

336. STODART.

GEORGE WASHINGTON. Half length, head to left. (Lansdowne.) *Stipple.*

Height 3 8-16 inches; width 3 inches.

Engraved by G. Stodart. *Published by J. Mason* 14 *City Road &* 66 *Paternoster Row.* *Rare.*

337. STRICKLAND.

Bust, head to left, on a pedestal partly hidden by an open scroll inscribed, "Constitution of the United States." An U. S. Shield on front of pedestal. Vignette. *Aquatint.*

Height 9 inches; width 6 8-16 inches.

Rare.

338. TANNER.

G. WASHINGTON. Bust, head to right. Oval, in a rectangle; the title, in a tablet below the oval. *Stipple.*

Height 3 3-16 inches; width 2 6-16 inches.

Tanner sc. "Engraved for the Revd M. L. Weems."

339. TANNER.

G^L WASHINGTON. Bust, head to right. Oval in a rectangle.

Stipple.

Height 3 3-16 inches; width 2 6-16 inches.

[The Life of George Washington with curious anecdotes equally honorable to himself and exemplary to his young countrymen. Tenth Edition. By M. L. Weems. Philadelphia, Printed for Mathew Carey, 1810.]

340. TANNER.

G. WASHINGTON. Bust, head to right. Oval. *Stipple.*

Height 4 8-16 inches; width 3 13-16 inches.

B. Tanner sc. *Rare.*

341. TANNER.

GEORGE WASHINGTON FIRST PRESIDENT OF THE UNITED STATES AND LATE LIEUTENANT GENERAL OF THE AMERICAN ARMIES. DIED AT Mr VERNON 14TH DEC^R 1799, aged 68 years. Full Bust in uniform, head to right; on the left breast, the order of the Cincinnati. *Stipple.*

Height 5 10-16 inches; width 4 9-16 inches.

B. Tanner sc.   *Very rare.*

342. THOMSON.

GEORGE WASHINGTON.   Full Bust, head to left.   *Stipple.*

Height 4 6-16 inches; width 3 8-16 inches.

Painted by G. Stuart.   Eng^d by J. Thomson.

343. TIEBOUT.

GEORGE WASHINGTON.   Full Bust, head to left.   Oval.   *Stipple.*

Height 8 13-16 inches; width 6 13-16 inches.

Painted by G. Stewart.   Engraved by C. Tiebout.   *Published by C. Tiebout N° 28 Gold Street New York January 8th 1800.*   *Rare.*

Cornelius Tiebout was the first American Engraver, to attain any excellence in his Art.   This print, is a good example of his abilities, although not a very close rendering of the original.

344. TIEBOUT.

GEORGE WASHINGTON.   Bust, head to left.   Oval.   *Stipple.*

Height 3 4-16 inches; width 2 8-16 inches.

G. Stewart Del.   C. Tiebout sculp.   *Rare.*

[Two Discourses occasioned by the Death of General George Washington.   By the Rev. Uzal Ogden, D.D.   Newark, 1800.]

345. TILLER.

GEN. GEO. WASHINGTON.   First President of the United States.   Bust, head to left.   Oval.   *Stipple.*

Height 8-16 inch; width 6-16 inch.

R. Tiller sc.   "Copyright secured."   *Very rare.*

In later impressions, surrounded by a wreath with diverging rays.

346. TOPHAM.

GENERAL WASHINGTON. Bust, head to right. (Lansdowne.)

Line.

Height 4 6-16 inches; width 3 4-16 inches.

Painted by G. Stuart. Engraved by S. Topham. *Leeds, Published by Davies & Booth.*

[History of North America comprising a Geographical and Statistical view of the United States. Leeds, 1820.]

347. WALMSLEY.

WASHINGTON. Bust, head to left. Oval, in a rectangle.

Mezzotinto.

Height 16 inches; width 13 2-16 inches.

Engraved by Samuel Walmsley after the original Painting taken from life by Gilbert Stuart.

348. WALTER.

GEORGE WASHINGTON. Full Bust, head to left. Oval.

Mezzotinto.

Height 8 2-16 inches; width 6 3-16 inches.

Eng⁴ by A. B. Walter. Painted by G. Stuart. *Published by John Dainty 31 S. 6ᵗʰ Str. Philadelphia.*

349. WEGER.

Half length, head to left, a scroll in the right hand, the arm resting upon the muzzle of a cannon. A sword in the left hand. Vignette.

Etched.

Height 4 5-16 inches; width 3 8-16 inches.

G. Longhi gez. A. Weger sc. Lpzg. *Verlag von Carl B. Lorck in Leipzig.*

The head, is a copy of the print by Longhi, No. 281.

21

350. WELCH.

G. WASHINGTON.   Half length, head to left.   *Mezzotinto.*

Height 5 3-16 inches; width 4 4-16 inches.

Engraved by T. B. Welch from a Portrait by G. Stuart.

[The Sages and Heroes of the American Revolution.   By L. Carroll Judson.   Philadelphia, 1851.]

351. WELCH.

WASHINGTON.   Head to left.   Vignette, with background ruled to a rectangle.   *Stipple.*

Height 22 14-16 inches; width 18 inches.

Engraved by Thomas B. Welch (By Permission), From the only original Portrait by Gilbert Stuart in the Athenæum, Boston.   *Published by George W. Childs, Philadelphia.*   (Copyright, 1852.)

The most important work of the engraver, and a very close rendering of the original. Welch was a fine draughtsman, and a painter, as well as an engraver.   A copy of this head by him in oil, which has come under the notice of the writer, is well executed and good in color.

352. WILLARD.

GEORGE WASHINGTON, INAUGURATED PRESIDENT 1789.   Bust, head to left.   Vignette.   *Stipple.*

Height 2 4-16 inches; width 2 2-16 inches.

[History of the United States.   By Rev. C. A. Goodrich.   Hartford, 1824.]

353. WOODRUFF.

WASHINGTON.   Bust, head to left.   Circular medallion, heading to an imperial folio sheet, containing "The Declaration of Independence," surrounded by fifteen smaller medallions, two of which contain Busts of Adams and Jefferson, the others, coats of arms of the thirteen original States.   *Line.*

Diameter 3 6-16 inches.

Engraved by Wm. Woodruff. *Philad⁺, Published Feb⁷ 20ᵗʰ 1819, by William Woodruff.*

354. WOOLLEY.

Bust, head to left. Oval, with border resting upon a base, in a folio sheet, surrounded by allegorical figures of History, Liberty, Immortality, Justice, and America. In the lower margin an Urn, and over it an Eagle with a laurel wreath. *Mezzotinto.*

Height 8 6-16 inches; width 7 inches.

Woolley pinxit et sculpsit. David Longworth Direxit. " This print from the original Picture in the Possession of Longworth and Wheeler, Is by them Dedicated to the memory of His Excellency Geo. Washington Esqʳ." *Published at the Shakespeare Gallery No 11 Park N. York.*
Extremely Rare.

Impressions of the oval with the Portrait alone, taken after the Border, Figures, &c., were removed, are common. The head is after Stuart.

355. WOOLLEY.

GEORGE WASHINGTON Esqr. Bust, head to left. Oval, in a rectangle. *Mezzotinto.*

Height 11 11-16 inches; width 10 inches.

Woolley pinxit et sculpsit. *Published at the Shakespeare Gallery No. 11 Park N. York.* *Extremely Rare.*

A copy of the Stuart head. Woolley engraved in the same style, a portrait of Mrs. Washington, as a companion print.

356. WRIGHT.

Bust, head to left. Oval, with border. *Line.*

Height 4 inches; width 3 8-16 inches.

Trott Delt. Wright engraver, N. Y.

357. WRIGHT.

WASHINGTON.   Bust, head to left.   Ornamented border representing
a picture frame.   *Line.*

Height 4 12-16 inches; width 4 inches.

358. —— ——.

GEORGE WASHINGTON.   Full length.   The "Lansdowne Portrait."
Fully described in the print by James Heath, No. 250.

Mezzotinto.

Height 25 6-16 inches ; width 19 6-16 inches.

Only one impression of this, has come under the notice of the writer.   It appears to
be the work of an English engraver of no particular merit, and probably executed about
the commencement of the century.

359. —— ——.

WASHINGTON.   Full length.   The "Lansdowne Portrait."   *Stipple.*

Height 8 inches; width 5 12-16 inches.

Only one impression of this, has come under the notice of the writer.   It is very rude
in execution, and the drawing bad in every respect.   An early American print.

360. —— ——.

Bust, head to right.   Oval, resting upon books labelled "ORDER, LAW,
RELIGION."   To the left, a lion, with fore feet on a scroll entitled
"Answer to Addresses," on the right, an eagle, head and neck only
visible, upon another scroll marked "Last Legacy."   At the top of
the oval, a laurel wreath with diverging rays.   To the right, in same
plate (Ob. 4to), an oval of like size, upon some books, containing the
portrait of Jefferson, facing.   The books are labelled "Sophism, Tom.
Paine, Voltaire, &c." with a rattlesnake and crocodile in place of the
lion and eagle.   In the lower margin, the quotation from Shakespeare,
"Look on this Picture and on this, &c. &c."   *Etched.*

Height 5 inches; width 4 inches.

New York, June, 1807.   *Extremely Rare.*

A political print and very well executed; no doubt by a foreign artist, as we know no American engraver of the time, equal to handling the point with such freedom. Only one complete impression has come under our notice, the Portrait of Washington in all other cases being found cut apart from the Jefferson.

361. —— ——.

GEORGE WASHINGTON First President of the United States and late Lieutenant General of the American Armies. Bust, head to left. Oval. *Stipple.*

Height 5 8-16 inches; width 4 8-16 inches.

Rare.

362. —— ——.

G. WASHINGTON Born Feb. 11ᵀᴴ (O. S.) 1732, Died Decʀ 14ᵀᴴ 1799. Full Bust, head to left. *Line.*

Height 8 14-16 inches; width 7 7-16 inches.

Rare.

363. —— ——.

GEO. WASHINGTON. Bust, head to right. Oval. *Stipple.*

Height 2 10-16 inches; width 2 inches.

Deare's Edition. Dedicated to the Washington Benevolent Societies in New Jersey. *Publish'd & Sold by Lewis Deare, N. Brunswick, N. Jersey.* *Rare.*

[Washington's Farewell Address to the People of the United States. New Brunswick 1813.]

364. —— ——.

GENᴸ GEORGE WASHINGTON. Full Bust, head to right, in the left distance, an encampment indistinctly seen. Oval. *Stipple.*

Height 3 6-16 inches; width 2 13-16 inches.

[The Life of George Washington with curious anecdotes &c. &c. By M. L. Weems. 25ᵗʰ Edition. Philadelphia, 1823.]

365. —— ——.

WASHINGTON. Bust, head to left. Circular. *Stipple.*

Diameter 3 10-16 inches.

Pub. by J. Price Jr. Philad^a.

[A New American Biographical Dictionary, Compiled by Thomas J. Rogers. Philadelphia, 1829.]

366. —— ——.

Bust, head to right. Oval. *Line.*

Height 1 14-16 inches; width 1 9-16 inches.

Title Page of "The Book of the Army of the United States. By John Frost L. L. D." *Appleton, New York.* 1845.

367. —— ——.

GEN. GEORGE WASHINGTON. BORN FEBRUARY 22ND 1732, AP-POINTED COMMANDER IN CHIEF OF THE AMERICAN ARMY JUNE 15TH 1775. ELECTED FIRST PRESIDENT OF THE UNITED STATES MARCH 4TH 1789. DIED 14TH DEC. 1799. Three quarter length sitting, in the right hand a book, and a dress sword lies in the left fore-arm. In the lower margin, the Washington arms. Oval, in a rectangle. *Stipple.*

Height 4 4-16 inches; width 3 4-16 inches.

Engraved from a copy after Stuart.

The picture was painted by Stuart in 1822.

368. —— ——.

Bust, head to right. Oval. *Line.*

Height 2 inches; width 1 10-16 inches.

Title Page of " A Pictorial History of the Wars of the United States. By John Ledyard Denison A. M. 1860."

369. —— ——.

GENERAL WASHINGTON, Late President of the United States of America. Half length, head to left. Oval, with border in a rectangle. *Mezzotinto.*

Height 12 inches; width 9 12-16 inches.

London, Published March 21st 1801 by Haines & Son, No. 19 Rolls Buildings, Fetter Lane.

Only one impression of this, has come under the notice of the writer.

370. —— ——.

GEORGE WASHINGTON, First President of the United States of America. Bust, head to left. In the background an open book case, with a window to the right. Vignette. *Stipple.*

Height 2 14-16 inches; width 2 6-16 inches.

Engraved from an original Picture in the possession of the Marquis of Lansdown. *London, William Darton 38 Holborn Hill, 1 mo. 28, 1824.* *Rare.*

371. —— ——.

GEORGE WASHINGTON First President of the United States of America. Full Bust, head to right. (Lansdowne.) Vignette. *Stipple.*

Height 3 8-16 inches; width 3 inches.

Published by G. Smeeton, St Martin's Church Yard.

372. —— ——.

GEORGE WASHINGTON. Bust, head to left. Border with lion's heads, in each corner. *Stipple.*

Height 3 inches; width 2 7-16 inches.

Published March 13, 1824 by George Smeeton, 3 Old Bailey.

373. —— ——.

GENERAL WASHINGTON. Full Bust, head to left.   *Stipple.*

Height 5 6-16 inches; width 4 11-16 inches.

London, Published by Richd Evans, 17 Paternoster Row

---

374. —— ——.

G. WASHINGTON. Bust, head to left. The background ruled perpendicular, and the corners rounded.   *Line.*

Height 4 inches; width 3 inches.

Gaspar Y. Roig Editores Madrid.

Only one impression of this, has come under the notice of the writer.

---

375. —— ——.

GEORGE WASHINGTON ESQ^R late President of the United
States of America. Full length standing, right hand upon a scroll
upon a table to the left, inscribed "Declaration of Independence."
To the right, an arm chair, and in the background a curtain drawn up
at the left, shows some pillars and the open sky.   *Mezzotinto.*

Height 18 inches; width 13 inches.

Engraved from an original Drawing by Savage.

Only one impression of this, has come under the notice of the writer. It has the
Stuart head, and in the general characteristics of the Figure and accessories, resembles
the "Tea Pot Portrait."

---

376. —— ——.

G. WASHINGTON. Half length, head to left. Upper corners rounded.
                                                     Line.

Height 5 4-16 inches; width 3 14-16 inches.

377. —— ——.

G. WASHINGTON. Full length. The "Lansdowne Portrait." Fully described in the print by James Heath No. 250. *Stipple.*

Height 19 14-16 inches; length 13 4-16 inches.

378. —— ——.

WASHINGTON. Bust, head to right. Oval. *Stipple.*

Height 3 7-16 inches; width 2 9 16 inches.

22

REMBRANDT PEALE.

1795.

THE second son of Charles Willson Peale, was born in Bucks County, Pa. (his mother having left Philadelphia on the approach of the British Army), on the twenty-second day of February, 1778, his Father at the time, being at Valley Forge.

At an early age, he imbibed a great veneration for the person and character of Washington, taking advantage of every opportunity which offered of seeing the First President, and when but eight years old (1786), stood behind his father's chair, while painting a portrait of him for his gallery, watching its progress, and the movements of the sitter's countenance, during his familiar conversation with the artist. This, surrounded as he was by art, and evincing considerable talent as a draughtsman, naturally grew into a controlling desire to paint the portrait of Washington himself, and in the autumn (September) of 1795, Washington, at the request of his father, consented to sit to him, but when the hour arrived the youthful aspirant found himself so much agitated, that he feared to attempt it unless his father would agree to take a canvas alongside of him.

Mr. Peale, during the winter of 1857–8, delivered a lecture in the principal cities of the United States, on "Washington and his Portraits", from a duplicate autograph copy of which, in the possession of Robert Coulton Davis, Esqr., of Philadelphia, we are permitted to make the following extracts, preferring to let the artist speak for himself:—

"Washington gave me three sittings. At the first and second, my father's painting and mine advanced well together; being at my right hand *his* was a little less full than *mine*. In the third sitting, perceiving that he was beginning to repaint the forehead and proceed downwards, as was his custom, I feared he would have too little time to study the mouth and lower part of the face, and therefore I began at the chin and proceeded upwards. The result of this decision was, that there was something in the upper part of my father's study that I preferred, and something in the lower portion of mine, which better satisfied me. At subsequent periods I made several studies to combine them. To profit more fully by the occasion, my uncle James Peale during the second and third sittings, painted at my left hand, a miniature on ivory, and for a time, my elder brother stood beyond my uncle, to make a profile sketch.

"Mrs. Washington happened to enter the room at the moment, and being amused by the circumstance, mentioned it to Stuart, who jocularly told her, she must take good care of her husband, as he was in danger of being *Peeled* all round.

"Washington gave me three sittings of three hours each, from 7 to 10. By these early visits, I had the advantage of seeing his hair in a more natural manner than the barber arranged it, wig-fashion, after 10 o'clock. In this particular, the hair in Col. Trumbull's portrait is much more easy and graceful, as he probably saw it in the negligence of a camp. He shaved himself before coming to me, and the powder being washed from the whiskers in front of his ears, showed that his hair was dark brown. What there was of gray on the top of his head, was disguised with powder; yet *there* his hair was abundant, and the plaited hair behind, was long and clubbed, to which was attached, on days of state ceremony, in dress of black velvet, the customary appendage of a black silk bag.

"My Portrait wet from the Easel, was packed up and in a few days was opened in Charleston, where I painted ten copies of it, which were valued as the most recent likeness. In executing these, I became familiar with whatever good it possessed, but also, became still more sensitive to its deficiencies.

"After the death of Washington neither satisfied with my father's nor Trumbull's, nor Pine's, nor Wertmuller's, nor Stuart's, nor my own, I made repeated attempts to fix on canvas, the Image which was so strong in my mind, by an effort of combination, chiefly of my father's, and my own studies.

"I had made during several years, sixteen of these attempts; and tho' not equal to my own expectation, they all found satisfied possessors. I determined in 1823, to make a last effort; and under an excitement even beyond the 'Poetic frenzy', which controlled me during three months, to the exclusion of every other thought, and to the grief of my father, who considered it a hopeless effort, I succeeded to his conviction."

This portrait, Mr. Peale carried abroad with him in 1829, exhibiting it in Naples, Rome, Florence, Paris, and London, and sold it after his return (1832), to the Government. It is in senatorial costume, and hangs in the Vice President's room in the Capitol at Washington. Mr. Peale, from time to time, made many copies of it (76). A portrait in military costume, the study for an equestrian picture to commemorate the Siege of Yorktown, was simultaneously painted, and from this also, he made careful copies. Mr. Peale also drew the head twice on the lithographic stone, one of which is larger than life.

Rembrandt Peale, studied in London under Benjamin West, between 1801 and 1804, and subsequently, passed some years in Paris, executing portraits of eminent men for his Father's Gallery. He died at Philadelphia, October 3, 1860.

The lithographic drawings by Peale being original works, are included in our list, the rule of admitting none but plate engravings, being very properly waived in such a case. The one first mentioned, is an exceedingly interesting production, admirably drawn, a fine example of the art, and a perfect fac-simile of the original painting. It is closely copied in the mezzotinto by Walter.

In a communication to William Dunlap, (Arts of Design vol 2 pa. 57), Mr. Peale has furnished the following facts, concerning this print, and his study of Lithography. "I was among the first of the artists who employed this admirable method of multiplying original drawings. My first attempt in New York, was a head of Lord Byron, and a female head from a work of Titian. In 1826, I went to Boston, and devoted myself for some time to lithographic studies, and executed a number of portraits and other subjects, and finally, a large drawing from my portrait of Washington, for which I obtained the silver medal from the Franklin Institute at Philadelphia, in 1827. Unfortunately, the workmen by some neglect, destroyed this drawing on the stone, when but a few impressions were taken."

The head by H. B. Hall executed in line, is a fine example of that engraver's abilities, and a close rendering of the original. The Portrait painted from life in 1795, has not been engraved. The prints in the appended list are after the one executed in 1823.

379. PEALE.

PATRIÆ PATER. Full Bust, head three quarters to right. Oval, with border surrounded by an oak wreath in a rectangle, the whole, imitating stone work. A cloak or mantle hangs over the front of the oval, with a colossal antique head as a Keystone. The Title, beneath the oval.

Lithograph.

Height 19 6-16 inches; width 15 6-16 inches.

Drawn on stone by Rembrandt Peale. Copyright secured 1827. *Pendleton's Lithography, Boston.* *Very Rare.*

380. PEALE.

WASHINGTON. Bust, head three quarters to right. *Lithograph.*

Height 23 inches; width 19 inches.

Drawn by Rembrandt Peale from his original Portrait. Copy Right secured 1856. *Duval & Co.*

381. HALL.

Bust, head three quarters to right. Vignette. *Stipple.*

Height 4 3-16 inches; width 4 inches.

Rembrandt Peale. H. B. Hall. *New York G. P. Putnam.*

[Life of George Washington. By Washington Irving. New York 1856–59.]

382. HALL.

WASHINGTON. Bust, head three quarters to right. Vignette. *Line.*

Height 4 3-16 inches; width 4 inches.

Eng⁴ by H. B. Hall, N. Y. 1865. After a painting by Rembrandt Peale.

[Washingtoniana, or Memorials of the Death of George Washington. By Franklin B. Hough. Roxbury, Mass., 1865.]

383. METZEROTH.

WASHINGTON BEFORE THE BATTLE OF YORKTOWN, GIVING ORDERS TO COMMENCE THE ENTRENCHMENTS, ACCOMPANIED BY LAFAYETTE, KNOX, LINCOLN, AND ROCHAMBEAU. Full figure in uniform, on horseback.

Line.

Height 3 inches; width 3 2-16 inches.

Rembrandt Peale pxt. R. Metzeroth sc.

384. WALTER.

G. WASHINGTON. Full Bust, head three quarters to right. Oval, with border surrounded by an oak wreath in a rectangle, the whole, engraved to represent stone work. A cloak or mantle, hangs over the front of the oval, with a colossal antique head as a Key-stone. Beneath the oval, the words "Patriæ Pater." *Mezzotinto.*

Height 19 inches; width 15 2-16 inches.

Rembrandt Peale pinx[t]. Adam B. Walter sculpt. *Published by C. N. Robinson No 248 Chestnut St. Philad[a].*

A close copy of the Lithograph No. 379.

WILLIAM BIRCH.

1796.

ENAMEL Painter and Engraver, was born in Warwick, England, and practiced in London. He exhibited at the Academy for the first time in 1781, and received the Society of Arts Medal in 1785, for excellence in his art, and improvements in the processes. In 1794, he came to the United States, and settled in Philadelphia. Birch executed a miniature in enamel of Washington, which according to the inscription on the engraving of it made by Walker, was painted (1796), from life, in the office of His Excellency The General, by the request of I. G. Van Staphorst, Esqr. of Amsterdam. It will be remembered, that the Van Staphorsts and the extensive mercantile house of John De Neufville & Son of Amsterdam, were firm friends of America, during the revolutionary struggle. The Artist, made several copies of this miniature.

William Birch died at Philadelphia, in 1834. Of the prints in the appended list, the one engraved by P. Roberts after a painting by "W. Birch of Carolina," and repeated as to the head, by W. Read, and in another without engraver's name, published at Paris by "Ménard & Desenne," presents a portrait, somewhat different from the miniature known to us, and from which, the engravings by Walker, Edwin, Hall, and the one printed on satin (no.391), engraver unknown, were executed. We have no knowledge of any other portrait painted by Birch, beside the miniature above referred to, and although the head in the Roberts print, does not bear much resemblance to it, have

(176)

presumed the lettering to be correct, and placed it in this connection. The engravings by Edwin and Hall and No. 391, are well executed, and are decidedly the best renderings of the miniature, the one by Walker, not being very good in that respect.

385. EDWIN.

GEO. WASHINGTON.   Full Bust, head three quarters to right.   Oval, with narrow border, in the upper part of a rectangle.   An eagle with laurel wreath, rests upon the top of the oval, and around the sides and base, are flags, laurel branches and war emblems.   Over the eagle, a circlet of ten stars.   The Title, in a tablet, in the rectangle.   *Stipple.*

Height 6 6-16 inches; width 3 13-16 inches.

Edwin sc.

[American Artillerist's Companion, or Elements of Artillery.   By Louis De Tousard.   Philadelphia, 1809.]

386. HALL.

Full Bust, head three quarters to right.   Vignette.   *Line.*

Height 3 8-16 inches; width 3 inches.

Eng⁴ by H. B. Hall, N. Y., from an original miniature by Wᵐ. Birch, in the Possession of Chas. G. Barney, Esqr.   (Private Plate.)

One hundred and twenty-five impressions taken, and the plate destroyed.

387. READ.

WASHINGTON.   Bust, head three quarters to right, the left hand thrust in the breast.   Vignette.   *Stipple.*

Height 2 inches; width 1 11-16 inches.

W. Read sc.   *London, Published Janʸ 9, 1823 by Sir R. Phillips & Co Bride Court, Bridge Street.*

23

388. ——— ———.

GEORGE WASHINGTON, Né à Bridges Creek le 22 Fevrier 1732, Mort le 14 Decembre 1799. Bust, head three quarters to right. Oval, with border, in the upper part of a rectangle, above a tablet in which is the Title.   *Line.*

Height 5 11-16 inches; width 3 11-16 inches.

A Paris, chez Ménard & Desenne, Rue Git-le-Cœur N° 8.

Proofs which are rare, have the title, "Washington," in open letters, the tablet without lines.

389. ROBERTS.

GEORGE WASHINGTON, Late President of the United States of America. Full Bust, head three quarters to right, the left hand thrust in the breast. Oval, with border resembling a picture frame, leaning against some rocks in a landscape, and surrounded by flags and war emblems. In the background, the rays of a setting sun. Oblong quarto sheet.   *Stipple.*

Height 4 inches; width 3 6-16 inches.

Painted by W. Birch, Esq., of Carolina. Engraved by P. Roberts. "This Plate is Humbly Dedicated to the Friends of the above Gentleman by their most obedient Humble Serv* P. Roberts." *London, Published as the act directs April* 10, 1800, *by P. Roberts at M*ʳ *Hollands.*
Rare.

390. WALKER.

HIS EXCEL*ʸ* GEN*ᴸ* GEO*ᴿ* WASHINGTON. Full Bust, head three quarters to right. The centre of an ornamented rectangle. Above, the Sun dispersing clouds, and beneath, a female figure with right hand on a bundle of fasces, and a child holding a pole, surmounted by a liberty cap.   *Line.*

Height 7 3-16 inches; width 5 10-16 inches.

Engraved by J. G. Walker From a Picture by W. Birch 1796. Painted from life in the office of His Excellency The General, by the request of I. G. Van Staphorst Esqʳ of Amsterdam, in whose possession the original Portrait now is. "To I. G. Van Staphorst Esqʳ the particular Friend of the General, This Print is with permission most respectfully Inscribed, by His obliged & obedt. Servant J. G. Walker." *Published as the act directs June 21*, 1800 *by Mr Bowyer Historic Gallery Pall Mall, Mr E. Wilkinson No 58 Cornhill, Mr Brewer the corner of Newgate Street & J. G. Walker Church Lane, Hammersmith.*

Proofs, which are extremely rare, two only having come under the notice of the writer, have the address as follows, in traced letters, "Publish'd as the Act directs June 16, 1800 by J. G. Walker, Hammersmith."

391. —— ——.

Full Bust, head three quarters to left. Oval. *Stipple.*

Height 5 12-16 inches; width 4 10-16 inches.

Only one impression of this has come under the notice of the writer. It is before all letters, and printed on satin, probably the production of an English engraver in the early part of the century.

392. —— ——.

Full Bust, head three quarters to left. Circle, surrounded by an outer line of laurel leaves, forming a border. *Stipple.*

Diameter 2 12-16 inches.

[The Columbiad, a Poem. By Joel Barlow. Paris, 1813.]

393. —— ——.

Bust, head three quarters to left. Oval, surrounded by a wreath, and inclosed by circular lines. Between the oval and the lines, the words "Columbian Total Abstinence Society." Beneath the Circle, "Aux. To Washington T. B. S." *Line.*

Height 1 12-16 inches; width 1 6-16 inches.

JAMES SHARPLESS.

1796.

An Englishman by birth, was educated in France, being intended for the priesthood in the Roman Catholic Church. He, however, preferred the Fine Arts, married after his return to England, and came to this country with his family about the year 1796, landing at New York. He painted in oil, but seems to have practiced mostly in crayons or pastils, which he manufactured for himself. Sharpless visited all the principal cities and towns in the United States, travelling in a four wheeled coach of his own contrivance, which carried the whole family, himself, wife and three children, and all his implements, and was drawn by one large horse.

His Portraits, executed usually in profile upon a small scale, include most of the distinguished persons of the time, and are valued for their character and truth.

When in Philadelphia in 1796, Sharpless drew a profile likeness in pastil of Washington, from life, which has been pronounced by members of the family most able to judge, as the best likeness extant. The artist made many copies from it, as did also Mrs. Sharpless, who painted miniatures in water colors.

James Sharpless died in New York, February 6, 1811, at the age of about sixty years.

The engraving by H. B. Hall, is the only one from this profile, although it has been reproduced several times on wood. It is well

(180)

executed, and is a fair rendering of the original drawing. A resemblance to this head is introduced into the Memorial Design, engraved
by Aikin & Harrison No. 400, a military coat, however, being added.

394. HALL.

G. WASHINGTON.   Head and Bust, in profile to left.   Vignette.

Line.

Height 3 inches; width 3 inches.

Eng^d by H. B. Hall, from a miniature painted from life by Sharpless,
in 1796.   (Private Plate.)

CHARLES BALTHAZAR JULIEN FEVRET DE SAINT MEMIN.

1798.

To whom we are indebted for the last portrait of Washington taken from life, was born at Dijon, France, on the 12th day of March, 1770, and quite early in life, showed an aptitude for design, and displayed considerable mechanical talent.

Destined for the profession of arms, he entered as a cadet at the military school in Paris, April 1, 1784, was appointed supernumerary Ensign in the following year, and Ensign April 27, 1788. His sympathies at the outbreak of the French Revolution, were with the Royal family, and the army of the Princes being formed, he joined it, and served in that organization until it was disbanded, at which time he was entitled to the rank of lieutenant-colonel, which was afterwards (Jan. 29, 1817), conferred upon him by Louis XVIII, taking grade from May 1, 1792. While with the army, he turned his attention, during his leisure hours, to drawing and painting.

He came to America from Switzerland, where he had learned to gild and carve in wood, landing in Canada in 1793, and from thence going to New York, in which city he learned to engrave.

Towards the end of the last century, a Frenchman named Chrétien, had invented a machine, by means of which he copied the human profile mathematically accurate. This invention, termed physionotracy, had great success. Saint Memin, knowing of the popularity of this process, practiced also by Queneday and others, determined to intro-

(182)

duce it into this country, and therefore applied himself to the construction of such a machine, according to his understanding of it, and also made a pantograph.

His profiles, were produced of life size by the physionotrace, and finished in crayon, the pantograph reducing them to the size required for the plate, the portrait being drawn on the copper, in a circle of a little more than two inches in diameter. Having thus obtained the perfect outline, the details were worked up by the graver, the shading being finished by the roulette, the latter tool made by a machine of his own invention.

These profile portraits produced very rapidly, number about eight hundred and twenty, and are interesting, most of them being likenesses of the prominent personages of the time, Saint Memin travelling to all the principal cities of the Union for that purpose, his summers being passed with the family at Burlington, N. J., where he executed the engravings. In this, he was assisted at first by a fellow-exile M. de Valnuit, and the plates produced previous to 1797, when Valnuit returned to France, bear both their signatures. These plates, became the property of the different sitters, Saint Memin retaining only a few impressions, for his private collection.

While in Philadelphia in 1798, Saint Memin secured a profile of Washington, who was in that city during the month of November, engaged in organizing the army for the threatened war with France. This drawing was not engraved at the time like the others, being as it would appear, an undertaking of his own, and was retained by him. It was purchased after his death, from his nephew and heir, and is now in the possession of J. Carson Brevoort, Esqr., of Brooklyn, N. Y.

It is a Bust in uniform, half life-size, drawn in crayon on tinted paper, is strikingly characteristic, and bears every evidence of originality. The engraving by Dudensing, is a fair rendering of this interesting profile, the last portrait of Washington, taken from life.

Saint Memin made a short visit to France in 1810, and returned finally in 1814. At the time of his decease, which occurred June 23, 1852, he was Director of the museum at Dijon, to which office he had been appointed July 27, 1817.

After his return to France, Saint Memin arranged the impressions retained by him of his different plates, in two sets, adding the names of the originals, which being done from memory, are not always correct. These sets purchased at the same time as the above mentioned drawing (November 1859), were brought to this country. One of them is in the "Corcoran Gallery of Art" Washington, and the other is owned by Elias Dexter of New York, who published photographic copies of them in 1862.

All of these prints except two of Washington, are of the same size. One of the Washington's is marked "Houdon," (the drawing, life-size, is also owned by Mr. Brevoort) and the other is founded on the drawing above referred to. The latter, an oval, quite small, is beautifully executed, and it is presumed was not outlined on the plate in his usual manner. This is the print first mentioned in the list.

395. SAINT MEMIN.

WASHINGTON.   Profile Bust, in uniform to right.   Oval.

Height 10-16 inch; width 8-16 inch.

Only three impressions of this original print, have come under the notice of the writer.

396. —— ——.

Profile Bust, in uniform to right.   Oval, surrounded by laurel branches, with diverging rays.   At the top, a pen and sword crossed, and beneath, on a ribbon "First in war, First in peace and First in the hearts of his Countrymen."   *Stipple.*

Height 10-16 inch; width 8-16 inch.

[Valedictory address of Washington to the People of the United States. Philadelphia, Pub. by Bradford & Inskeep; Inskeep & Bradford, New York, & William McIlhenny, Boston. Preface dated 1810.]   *Extremely rare.*

A remarkably close copy of the preceding print.

397. DUDENSING.

GEORGE WASHINGTON.   Bust in uniform, in profile to left.   Vignette.   *Stipple.*

Height 3 4-16 inches; width 3 inches.

From the original Portrait done in Crayon by C. B. J. F. de St. Memin, and now 1866, in the possession of J. Carson Brevoort Esqr. *Elias Dexter, 564 Broadway, New York.*

SILHOUETTES.

Of this style of Portraiture, so popular a century ago, there appear to be only two examples of our subject, at least known to the writer, which have been reproduced through the plate of the engraver. In the last years of the Presidency, an interesting one of this character was taken by Samuel Powel, Mayor of Philadelphia (1775 & 1789), traced on the wall by a shadow thrown from an Argand lamp, which had just then been invented. This, slightly reduced in size, was reproduced on stone, for the "American Historical and Literary Curiosities," Second Series, By John J. Smith, and is now in possession of the Massachusetts Historical Society, and published considerably smaller, by the Heliotype process, in their proceedings of 1873-'75.

Another cut with scissors, by Miss De Hart of Elizabethtown, N. J. 1783, is well known through its publication on wood, in Irving's Life of Washington. It is extremely unlike any known profile of Washington.

Both of the prints in our list, give characteristic profiles, and on that account are quite interesting.

(186)

398. —— ——.

GEO. WASHINGTON ESQ[R] PRESIDENT OF THE UNITED STATES. Bust in uniform, profile to left. Vignette.

Height 2 8-16 inches; width 1 12-16 inches.

From his Profile taken in 1791. *Published by J. Easton, Salisbury,* 1796.

[An Excursion to the United States of North America in the Summer of 1794. By Henry Wansey, F.A.S. Salisbury, 1796.]

Later impressions, have the Title, "General Washington President of the United States."

399. —— ——.

Bust in uniform, profile to right. Surrounded by a border, Grecian pattern; at the top, a ribbon tied into a bow.

Height 3 12-16 inches; width 3 2-16 inches.

Only one impression of this, has come under the notice of the writer.

MEMORIAL DESIGNS.

UNDER this head, will be found such portraits as have been introduced into designs, commemorative of the death and virtues of one, of whom it has been said, that "Until time shall be no more, will a test of the progress which our race has made in wisdom and in virtue, be derived, from the veneration paid to the immortal name of Washington."

These designs, mostly monumental in character, were published shortly after the decease of Washington, and have now become with one or two exceptions, extremely rare. They are very interesting as evidences of the deep undercurrent of feeling at the time, which sought expression in every available manner. All the engravings in this list, were executed by American engravers.

None of the portraits, are very close to any original, although it has been thought proper as a guide, to indicate in the descriptions, such types as the designer no doubt intended to convey.

400. AIKIN & HARRISON.

AMERICA LAMENTING HER LOSS AT THE TOMB OF WASHINGTON. INTENDED AS A TRIBUTE OF RESPECT PAID TO DEPARTED MERIT & VIRTUE IN THE REMEMBRANCE OF THAT ILLUSTRIOUS HERO & MOST AMIABLE MAN WHO DIED DEC. 14, 1799. Profile Bust, in uniform, to right. Oval medallion, upon the shaft of a Monument, surmounted by a funereal urn. Over the medallion, a wreath, and beneath, "G. Washington." Upon a tablet, the following inscription.

(188)

Born 11ᵗʰ Feby O. S., 1732.
Com. Cont. Army, 1775.
Pres. Fed. Convention, 1787.
Pres. United States, 1789.
Declined Election, 1796.
Com. Fed. Army, 1798.

America, represented by a female figure leaning upon the base of the Monument, to the right. On either side, cypress and willow trees, and in the immediate foregound, an eagle with bowed head. *Line.*

Height 11 12-16 inches; width 7 6-16 inches.

Design'd, Engraved & Published, by Aikin & Harrison Junʳ, Philadᵃ Janʸ 20ᵗʰ 1800.

Only two impressions of this, have come under the notice of the writer. The profile resembles the Sharpless Portrait.

401. ECKSTEIN.

FULL FIGURE, in uniform, standing upon a pedestal, head to right, a baton in the extended right hand, the left, resting lightly upon the sword hilt at his side. The coat is buttoned, with the order of the Cincinnati on the left. On the left of the figure, a bundle of fasces against the trunk of a tree, upon a branch of which is a cocked hat. In the background, and to the right and left, representations of various battles. Upon the pedestal engraved to imitate marble, "First in war, First in Peace, and First in the Hearts of his Country." (Head after Stuart.) *Stipple.*

Height 23 4-16 inches; width 18 13-16 inches.

Design'd, Engrav'd & Publish'd, by John Eckstein Philadᵃ. "To the Honorable the Society of the Cincinnati, this Monument of Genˡ George Washington, Is very respectfully inscribed by the artist."

Extremely rare.

402. EDWIN.

APOTHEOSIS OF WASHINGTON. Full figure seated on clouds, a cherub in the act of crowning him with a laurel wreath. Beneath, to the right, a view of the Mansion at Mount Vernon. *Stipple.*

Height 20 14-16 inches; width 14 10-16 inches.

Painted by R. Peal. Engrav'd by Edwin. *Published by S. Kennedy, N° 129 Chesnut St. corner of 4th, Philadelphia.* *Rare.*

403. GRIDLEY.

PATER PATRIÆ. Bust in uniform, head three quarters to right. Oval medallion, upon the shaft of a Monument pyramidal in shape, surmounted by a funereal urn. The medallion is supported by Minerva, and Fame holds over it by her left hand, a laurel wreath which encircles the title; in her mouth a trumpet, from which hangs a banner inscribed TRENTON, PRINCETOWN, MONMOUTH, YORKTOWN. In a tablet upon the base, to which the Genius of America is pointing with averted head, the inscription in seven lines, "Sacred to the memory of the truly Illustrious George Washington, Renowned in War, Great in the Senate, and possessed of every Qualification to render him worthy the Title of a Great and Good man." Upon the plinth, "Born Feb. 22, 1732, Ob. Dec. 14, 1799." In the right foreground, a soldier wearing a conical shaped hat, is expressing grief, his gun upon the ground. The Genii of War, Liberty and Truth with emblems, surround the shaft. (Head after Savage.) *Line.*

Height 13 inches; width 8 14-16 inches.

Painted by John Coles jun. Eng⁴ by E. G. Gridley. (Boston, July 28, 1800.) *Extremely rare.*

404. MAVERICK.

GEN. GEORGE WASHINGTON DEPARTED THIS LIFE DECᴿ 14ᵀᴴ 1799. Æ. 67. AND THE TEARS OF A NATION WATERED HIS GRAVE. Full Bust in uniform, head to right. Oval, with border; in the upper half of the border, the words "Sacred to the memory of the brave," in the lower half, eighteen stars. The oval rests on a base, upon which the lines,

"Washington's no more, by silence grief's express'd,
Lo! here he lies, his works proclaim the rest."

A medallion upon the base, contains the title &c, in eight lines.

Stipple.

Height 4 12-16 inches; width 4 3-16 inches.

P. Maverick. Newark, N. Jersey.

From a folio sheet, containing verses &c engraved in script, entitled "Eulogium, sacred to the memory of the Illustrious George Washington, Columbia's Great and successful son, Honored be his name." Designed, written and Published, by Benjamin O. Tyler, Professor of Penmanship, New York 1815. The head is after Stuart.

405. SEYMOUR.

In Memory of GEN[L] GEORGE WASHINGTON and his Lady. Busts of Washington and Mrs. Washington, facing each other, upon a large funereal urn on a pedestal, placed in a landscape beneath a weeping willow. Washington in uniform, head three quarters to right. In the back-ground, a view of the Mansion House and out buildings at Mt. Vernon. Three figures, two of whom are females (one weeping), are advancing from the left. (The head resembles Savage.)   *Stipple.*

Height 11 5-16 inches; length 16 8-16 inches.

S. Seymour Fecit. *Philad[a] Jan.* 1, 1804, *Published by J. Savage according to Law.*

406. TANNER.

COMMEMORATION OF WASHINGTON. Full Figure, surrounded by clouds rising from a tomb, supported by Time and Immortality, the latter pointing upwards. To the left, figures of Faith, Hope and Charity. In the fore-ground to the right, an Indian with bowed head, and to the left, Liberty with war emblems at her feet. On the tomb, the inscription "Sacred to the Memory of Washington, Ob. 14 Dec. A. D. 1799 Æt. 68." I. J. Barralet Fecit.   *Stipple.*

Height 24 inches; width 18 6-16 inches.

Philadelphia, Published by Simon Chaudron and John J. Barralet. Jan[r] 1802.

Later impressions printed in tint, have, "Drawn and engraved by J. J. Barralet" and "Published 22nd Feby. 1816 by B. Tanner Engraver N° 74 South Eighth Street Philadelphia."

407. TIEBOUT.

GEO. WASHINGTON. Full figure in uniform, upon a pedestal, in the middle distance of the design. In the right hand, an open scroll inscribed "Friends and Fellow citizens," the left, upon a sword at his side. Army and navy emblems on each side of the pedestal, upon which is the title. In the immediate fore-ground in front of the statue, a large funereal urn upon a pedestal, on which in a tablet, "Sacred to Patriotism." In the back-ground, a view of Bowling Green, New York.

Line.

Height 16 10-16 inches; width 10 4-16 inches.

Designed & Drawn by Chas. Buxton M.D. Tiebout sculp.

Only one impression of this, has come under the notice of the writer. The head is after Stuart.

408. —— ——.

BUST, head to right, in an oval medallion (1 8-16 $\times$ 1 2-16) upon a Pyramid in the middle distance, over which a figure of Fame with trumpet. In the immediate fore-ground, an urn beneath which, the words "Born Feby. 11, 1732 O. S. Died Decemb. 16th 1799. Lived, respected and Fear'd, Died, Lamented and rever'd." On the right a figure of Justice, and on the left Columbia lamenting. Palm trees on either side.

Line.

Height 10 6-16 inches; width 9 12-16 inches.

"Columbia, lamenting the loss of her son,
Who redeem'd her from Slavry & Liberty won,
While Fame, is directed, by Justice to spread,
The sad tidings afar, that Washington's dead."

Philadelphia, Publish'd by Pember & Luzardes, 1800.

Only one impression of this, has come under the notice of the writer. The head is after Stuart.

FICTITIOUS PORTRAITS.

THE prints included in this list, with the exception of those by Holl and Laugier, in both of which the Stuart head is introduced, and the one in armor, which indicates the Peale Portrait, seem to have been made to order, either in the case of the smaller ones, for careless publishers, or in regard to the larger, created at the whim of the painter or engraver.

In one or two, such as that engraved by Chapman and the one published in the Emigrant's Directory, which is a copy of the head in the print by Bell, they are without doubt, actual portraits of other personages, the name of Washington being substituted on the plate, in lieu of the correct one. The book-plate published by Symonds, London, 1796, representing an elderly gentleman in full dress, in the posture of a dancing master, and awkward at that, was perhaps intended as a caricature on the supposed inability of any American, to appear properly in polite society, the name of Washington as President, being affixed, to give it more point.

The print by Best, after a painting by Christian Schussele, representing Washington at Valley Forge, with the Duché letter, is very well engraved. Those by Perine and Walter, "Washington as a Mason," are after the same picture, but we have no information as to the artist.

409. BAKER.

WASHINGTON Crossing the Delaware. Full figure in uniform, on horseback, military cloak and chapeau with cockade, advancing to the right. A field glass drawn fully out, in the right hand. The horse is richly caparisoned, the holster covered with a large rosette, upon which is the letter W. The background is formed from heavy masses of rock, and through an opening to the left, soldiers are advancing. To the right, a view of the river, with the troops crossing in boats. *Etched.*

Height 15 inches; width 12 10-16 inches.

I. Baker. Entered according to act of Congress by H. Phelps, in the office of the Clerk of the Dist. Ct. of the U. S. for the Southern Dis* of N. Y.

Only one impression of this, has come under the notice of the writer.

410. BAKER.

WASHINGTON (crossing the Delaware). Full figure, in uniform and chapeau, on horseback advancing to the right, an extended field glass in his right hand. In the rear to the right, the river, and troops crossing and preparing to cross. Without sky or inclosing lines. *Etched.*

Height 13 8-16 inches; width 12 inches.

Published by Humphrey Phelps, 336 Bowery & 157 Broadway N. York, Aug^{st} 1st 1833. *Extremely rare.*

An entirely different print, from the preceding one.

411. BELL.

THE WASHINGTON FAMILY. Full length, in uniform and chapeau, standing upon a portico at the head of a flight of steps, taking leave of Mrs. Washington preparatory to a ride. A riding whip in the left hand, the right extended towards Mrs. Washington, who stands about the centre of the print. A negro groom in waiting with a saddle horse, at the extreme right. Three young people, a boy and two girls, one of whom is seated, are at the left. To the right, the view of a distant landscape. *Mezzotinto.*

Height 17 12-16 inches; width 23 11-16 inches.

Painted by J. Paul Jun ͬ Philadelphia. Engraved by E. Bell London. *Published December 1ˢᵗ 1800, by Atkins and Nightingale Nᵒ 143 Leadenhall Street London & No. 35 North Front Street, Philadelphia.*

Extremely rare.

412. —— ——.

GENERAL WASHINGTON. Bust, in uniform and chapeau, head three quarters to left. Vignette. *Stipple.*

Height 4 inches; width 3 inches.

Published as the act directs for I. Sumner & Co. Shakespeare Press, Wigan.

[Emigrant Directory. London, 1820.]

This head, the same as in the preceding print, was also engraved (in stipple), to the right; the centre of an oblong quarto sheet, with the heads of Locke, Newton, Pope and another in each corner.

413. BEST.

G. WASHINGTON. Full length in uniform, seated at a table upon which is a military cloak. Head to right. A sword rests against the chair, and a letter is held in the right hand. *Line.*

Height 21 8-16 inches; width 16 7-16 inches.

Painted by C. Schussele. Engraved by Edward S. Best.

This plate, has not been properly lettered. The correct title is " WASHINGTON AND THE DUCHÉ LETTER, VALLEY FORGE 1777."

414. BROWN.

WASHINGTON. Full figure in uniform (overcoat), on horseback, advancing to the front, head in profile to right. A chapeau in the extended right hand, the left on the breast, as if receiving a salute.

Etched.

Height 5 3-16 inches; width 4 2-16 inches.

J. L. Brown sc. *Paris, Cadart & Luce Editeurs, Imprimeurs, Rue N^{ve} des Mathurins* 58.

415. CHAPMAN.

GEORGE WASHINGTON. Bust, in uniform and chapeau, head three quarters to right. Oval. *Stipple.*

Height 3 inches; width 2 6-16 inches.

R. K. Porter Delin. J. Chapman sculp^t. Engraved for Mackenzie & Dent's Select Biography.

This was also printed in tint.

416. HOLL.

WASHINGTON RECEIVING A SALUTE ON THE FIELD OF TRENTON. Full figure, in uniform on horseback, advancing to the right, a drawn sword in extended right hand. His hat resting in the fore-arm, is held by the left hand. *Line.*

Height 24 inches; width 17 10-16 inches.

John Faed R. S. A. Wm Holl. *Published exclusively for Subscribers, by the "National Art Association."* New York 1865.

An admirable engraving, of an admirable picture. The horse, which is exceedingly well drawn, is said to have been painted by R. Ansdell, the composition of the picture being by Faed. Head after Stuart.

417. LAUGIER.

WASHINGTON. Full length, in uniform standing, head to left, a field glass in the right hand. To the left a mounted cannon, and to the right partly in the rear, a horse led by a soldier. In the distance to the left, on the opposite bank of a river, fortifications. *Line.*

Height 25 4-16 inches; width 21 inches.

Engraved by Laugier 1839. Painted by Cogniet 1836. "The head from the original Painting by G. Stuart in the Athenæum, Boston."

418. —— ——.

HIS EXCELLENCY GEORGE WASHINGTON ESQ[R] Captain General of all the American Forces. Full length, in uniform and cocked hat, a baton in the extended right hand, while the left rests upon the muzzle of a cannon. Head, nearly in profile to left. In the left distance, a commander's marquee and tents. *Line.*

Height 6 12-16 inches; width 4 inches.

[An Impartial History of the War in America between Great Britain and Her Colonies from its Commencement to the end of the year 1779. London & Carlisle 1780.]

Impressions of this plate occur, taken after the sky, tents and marquee, were removed. They show considerable wear.

419. NORMAN.

HIS EX[cy] GEORGE WASHINGTON ESQ. Captain General of all the American Forces. Full length, in uniform and cocked hat, a field glass in the extended right hand, and resting by the left upon the muzzle of a large cannon. *Line.*

Height 6 inches; width 3 14-16 inches.

J. Norman sc. *Extremely rare.*

[An Impartial History of the War in America between Great Britain and the United States from its Commencement to the end of the War. Boston, 1781–82.]

Copy of the preceding print.

420. PERINE.

WASHINGTON as a Mason. Full length standing, in Masonic Regalia, the right hand on an upright book (upon a table), labelled "Ancient Masonic Constitutions," the left, holds a mallet upon a pedestal. Oval. *Mezzotinto.*

Height 8 3-16 inches; width 6 3-16 inches.

Eng[d] by Geo. E. Perine. From a Photograph. *Published by Moore & Co. 111 Nassau St. New York.*

421. PINHAS.

GEORG. WASHINGTON. Full figure, in uniform and chapeau, on horseback advancing to the left, a drawn sword in extended right hand. A palm tree in the background to the left, and some negroes and low buildings in the right. The landscape southern in character. *Line.*

Height 5 14-16 inches; width 4 inches.

H. Pinhas sc. *Extremely rare.*

422. SASSO.

GIORGIO WASHINGTON. Full length, standing on the bank of a river, right hand in the breast, the left, the arm parallel with the body, open the palm downwards. On the right, two male figures, one about entering a small boat. To the left, a palm tree.

Height 6 12-16 inches; width 4 10-16 inches.

G. B. Bosio dis. G. A. Sasso inc.

Only one impression of this, has come under the notice of the writer.

423. SCOTT.

GENERAL WASHINGTON. Bust, head nearly in profile to right.

Line.

Height 3 8-16 inches; width 2 8-16 inches.

R. Scott sc. *Rare.*

424. —— ——.

GEN^{L} WASHINGTON. Bust, head nearly in profile to right. Inclosed by an ornamental border, the sides being pillars around which oak branches are wreathed. In front of the base, upon which the pillars rest (and in which is the title) a helmet, with a sword and burning torch crossed. *Line.*

Height 6 inches; width 4 inches.

Published by W. Lockhead Printer, Berwick.

[Travels in and History of America; including the United States, with the British settlements &c. &c. Abridged and compiled by Dr. Reid. Berwick, n. d.]

This is the preceding plate, the engraver's name erased, and the border, ornaments &c added.

425. WALTER.

WASHINGTON AS A MASON. Full length standing, in Masonic Regalia, the right hand on an upright book (upon a table), labelled "Ancient Masonic Constitutions," the left holds a mallet upon a pedestal. Oval.

Mezzotinto.

Height 8 2-16 inches; width 6 3-16 inches.

Eng⁴ by A. B. Walter. *Published by John Dainty 15 S. 6ᵗʰ St. Philadelphia.*

426. —— ——.

THE TRUE PORTRAITURE OF HIS EXCELLENCY GEORGE WASHINGTON ESQᴿ IN THE ROMAN DRESS, AS ORDERED BY CONGRESS FOR THE MONUMENT TO BE ERECTED IN PHILADELPHIA, TO PERPETUATE TO POSTERITY THE MAN WHO COMMANDED THE AMERICAN FORCES THROUGH THE LATE GLORIOUS REVOLUTION. Full length, clad in complete armor, excepting a glove and helmet on the ground at the left. The right hand ungloved holds a lance or flag staff, which extends from the upper to the lower edge of the print. In the right background, the representation of a battle. (The head resembles Peale.) *Line.*

Height 9 4-16 inches; width 7 4-16 inches.

Shortly after the proclamation of peace, Congress passed a resolution, that an equestrian statue of Washington, should be erected, that it should be of bronze, and the General to be represented in a Roman Dress, holding a truncheon in his right hand, and his head encircled with a laurel wreath. This print, which is said to be a copy of one in Guillim's Heraldry, 5ᵗᵇ Edition, London, 1679, the head of Washington being inserted, was no doubt published at the time, in burlesque of the resolution. Only one impression, has come under the notice of the writer.

427. —— ——.

GEORGE WASHINGTON Președent of the United States of America. Full figure in civil dress, head to left, a medallion on his breast, suspended by a ribbon around his neck. In the right hand a cocked hat, the left by the side holds a dress sword in an awkward manner. Inclosed by a narrow border, in which at the top is a roll crossed by a pen, inscribed "Revolution." No background.　　　*Line.*

Height 6 inches; width 4 4-16 inches.

Published by H. D. Symonds, June 18, 1796.　　　*Extremely rare.*

428. —— ——.

GEOᴱ WASHINGTON ESQᴿ Commander in chief of the Forces & late President of the United States of America. Full Bust in uniform, in profile to left. Oval.　　　*Line.*

Height 3 10-16 inches; width 2 14-16 inches.

London, Published by G. Cawthorn, British Library 132 *Strand,* 31 *June,* 1799.

429. —— ——.

GEO. WASHINGTON. Full Bust in uniform, in profile to right. Oval.
　　　Stipple.
Height 4 3-16 inches; width 3 6-16 inches.

Engraved for the Ladies Mag.

430. —— ——.

GEORGE WASHINGTON ESQᴿ. Bust, head nearly in profile to left. Oval.　　　*Line.*
Height 3 5-16 inches; width 2 9-16 inches.

Published by G. Kearsley, Fleet St. May 1, 1800.　　　*Rare.*

[British Magazine, Vol. 1, Jany. to July, 1800. A sketch of the Life of the late General Washington. By John Corry.]

431. —— ——.

GEORGE WASHINGTON Late President of the United States of America &c. Full length standing, head three quarters to right, the left hand upon an open scroll upon a table to the right. The right hand behind his back, holds a hat only partly visible. An open window with a curtain drawn up, in the background. *Mezzotinto.*

Height 12 11-16 inches; width 9 14-16 inches.

Publish'd March 14, 1801, *by I. Hinton,* 44 *top of Wells Str[t], Oxford Strt.*

Only one impression of this, has come under the notice of the writer.

432. —— ——.

GEN[L] WASHINGTON. Bust in uniform, head nearly in profile to right. Vignette, surrounded by a single circular line of laurel wreath.

Printed in tint.

Diameter 1 10-16 inches.

Only one impression of this, has come under the notice of the writer.

433. —— ——.

GENERAL WASHINGTON. Full figure in uniform and chapeau, on horseback advancing to the right, a drawn sword in the right hand. The horse has a long flowing tail, which touches the ground. Inclosed by a single line for border, no background. *Line.*

Height 5 2-16 inches; width 4 4-16 inches.

Sold by C. Sheppard, Lambert Hill, Doctors Commons.

Extremely rare.

434. —— ——.

GENERAL WASHINGTON Father and Protector of America. Full length standing, the left hand on hip, the right arm extended. In the background a curtain, and to the left two pillars upon a large base.

Mezzotinto.

Height 12 8-16 inches; width 9 12-16 inches.

Only one impression of this, has come under the notice of the writer. An imitation of the full length by Stuart, the " Lansdowne Portrait."

26

STATUARY.

As none of these pieces, except the statue produced by Houdon, and the bust by Ceracchi, both of which will be found in the body of the work, can be classed as real portraits,—the aim of the artist being rather to present an idea,—we mention but briefly, such engravings as have come under our notice, without any effort to furnish a list, either complete or descriptive.

BERNARDI, JACOPO.	HORATIO GREENOUGH.	Seated figure. Folio. *Line.*
BERTINI, AUG.	ANTONIO CANOVA.	Seated figure. Folio. *Line.*
HALL, GEO. R.	THOMAS CRAWFORD.	Equestrian. Quarto. *Line.*
HALL, GEO. R.	H. K. BROWN.	Equestrian. Quarto. *Mixed.*
MARCHETTI, DOM.	ANTONIO CANOVA.	Seated figure. Folio. *Line.*
MOSES, HENRY.	ANTONIO CANOVA.	Seated figure. Octavo. *Outline.*
NORMAND.	F. CHANTREY.	Standing figure. Octavo. *Outline.*
ROGERS, JOHN.	CLARK MILLS.	Equestrian. Quarto. *Line.*
THOMSON, J.	F. CHANTREY.	Standing figure. Folio. *Stipple.*

APPENDIX.

CHARLES WILLSON PEALE.

IN the sketch of this Artist, attention was called (page 14), to an advertisement in "The Pennsylvania Packet," of August 26, 1780, relative to a print of Washington published by him, executed in mezzotinto after a portrait painted for the Executive Council of the State of Pennsylvania, and that up to the time of writing, no impression of it had come under our notice.

Through information furnished by Mr. John A. McAllister of Philadelphia, we have since been enabled to examine an impression of this plate, in the possession of Mrs. Robert B. Cabeen of Germantown, in whose family it has been from the time of its publication. The picture is a repetition in reverse—the accesories slightly varied,—of the full length commenced by Peale at Valley Forge and engraved by Wolff. The plate is well engraved. We furnish the following description.

PEALE.

HIS EXCELLENCY GEORGE WASHINGTON ESQUIRE, COMMANDER IN CHIEF OF THE FEDERAL ARMY. Nearly three quarter length in uniform standing, resting by the right hand upon a field piece to the left. The left hand holding a hat is upon his hip. In the background to the right, Nassau Hall, Princeton, and in the rear to the left a flag with thirteen stars, and an attendant with a horse, the head only visible.

Mezzotinto.

Height 11 14-16 inches; width 9 14-16 inches.

Chaᵗ Willson Peale pinxᵗ et fecit. This Plate is humbly Inscribed to the Honorable the Congress of the United States of America. By their Obedient Servant, Chaᵗ Willson Peale.

MADAME de BREHAN.

In the sketch of this Artist, page 68, allusion is made to the earliest engraving from the profile executed by her, an impression of which was presented by Washington to Mrs. Robert Morris; with the statement that the engraving by Charles Burt, No. 114, was copied from this, but that the writer had been unable to see the print, and was not aware of the name of the engraver.

Though the kindness however of Mr. Burt, we have now before us a photograph of this print, presumed to be of the same size as the original, from which we furnish, according to the plan of our work, the following description. The name of the engraver being quite indistinct, and it not appearing in any book, we do not vouch for its accuracy.

SÉRAENT.

GEORGE WASHINGTON. Profile head to right, laureated. Circular medallion, suspended by a ring and ribbon. The title in the upper part of the border. *Stipple.*

Diameter 3 6-16 inches.

Gravé d'apres le Camèe, peint par Mᵐᵉ la Marquise de Bréant, par A. F. Séraent, 1790.

INDEX.

INDEX TO ENGRAVERS.

27

AMERICAN ENGRAVERS REPRESENTED IN THE WORK.

Aikin, James.
Anderson, Alexander.
Andrews, Joseph.
Baker, I.
Balch, V.
Bannister, J.
Bather, G. J.
Best, Edward S.
Burt, Charles.
Buttre, J. C.
Casilear, John W.
Chorley, John.
Clarke, T. C.
Daggett, A.
Dodd, S.
Doolittle, Amos.
Doney, Thomas.
Dudensing, R.
Durand, Asher B.
Eckstein, John.
Edwin, David.
Fairman, Gideon.
Ferris, Stephen G.
Field, Robert.
Forrest, Ion B.
Gimber, S. H.
Gimbrede, Thomas.
Gobrecht, Christian.
Goodman, Charles.
Gridley, E. G.
Hall, Henry B.
Hall, George R.
Hall, Alice.
Halpin, John.
Hamlin, William.
Harrison, Charles P.

Harrison, Jr., William.
Hatch, George W.
Hill, S.
Hills, J. H.
Houston, H.
Humphreys, William.
Illman, Thomas.
Jocelyn, S. S.
Johnston, D. C.
Kelly, Thomas.
Kennedy, J.
Kimberly, D.
Kneass, W.
Lawson, Alexander.
Leney, William S.
Longacre, James B.
Marshall, William E.
Maverick, Peter.
McCarty, ———.
McRae, John C.
Murray, George.
Norman, J.
O'Neill, J. A.
Ormsby, William L.
Paradise, J. W.
Parker, George.
Peale, Charles Willson.
Pekenino, Michele.
Pelton, Oliver.
Perkins, Jacob.
Perkins, Joseph.
Perine, George E.
Piggot, Robert.
Pilbrow, ———.
Prud'homme, J. F. E.
Rawdon, Ralph.

Reed, Abner.
Rice, James R.
Rice, E. A.
Ritchie, A. H.
Roberts, John.
Robin, Augustus.
Rogers, John.
Rollinson, William.
Sadd, H. S.
St Memin, C. B. J. F. de.
Sartain, John.
Sartain, William.
Savage, Edward.
Scoles, I.
Seymour, Samuel.
Smith, John R.
Smith, G. G.
Smith, H. Wright.
Soper, R.
Steel, James W.
Strickland, William.
Tanner, Benjamin.
Tiebout, Cornelius.
Tiller, R.
Tisdale, E.
Trenchard, J.
Tucker, William E.
Walmsley, Samuel.
Walter, Adam B.
Warner, William.
Welch, Thomas B.
Willard, A.
Woodruff, William.
Woolley, ———.
Wright, C. C.
Wright, Joseph.